"An irreverent and provocative look at leadership from an experienced coach — it should set you thinking about how you can make a difference as a more considered leader."

Rob Goffee, Professor of Organisational Behaviour, London Business School

"Dan takes and interesting and unique look at leadership in this book — it makes a change to look at this subject through a negative lens that then creates a positive output."

Clive Smith, Head of Talent & Leadership Development, Barclays UK Retail Bank

"Terrible leaders are all around us. They are the business 'leaders' who have been ruining corporations and betraying the trust of shareholders, from Enron to Lehman Brothers, bringing western capitalism to its knees. They are the political 'leaders' who were oppressing populations in the Middle East and North Africa for decades, as well as the sorry, bumbling British politicians who can't tell the difference between a salary and an expense claim. And, perhaps most frightening of all, they are the mass of people who go to the office, check their personality, common sense and basic humanity at the door, and then get to work...

Dan White does us all a great service. He explains, in a lively, witty and intelligent book, what terrible leadership is. He provides examples (from Ivan t!

GW00545599

describes what is in the mind of those people that choose to follow the dark side. This book is for those people who have ever been the victims of terrible leadership, or who have ever considered acting in their own self-interest, or who simply want to be better leaders themselves. It is, in other words, for everyone.

The Terrible Leader is a satire — a book that would be understood and appreciated by writers from Jonathan Swift to Peter Cook and Scott Adams — but it's also a guide to the great as well as the ghastly. Dan White's insight into terrible leadership is fascinating and strangely seductive, as well as funny and enlightening. Perhaps that's the point: terrible leadership isn't simply an absolute, it's also a spectrum of behaviour. We can drift into it, sometimes without even knowing.

So, just in case you're in any doubt, great leadership sounds like this: "We choose to go to the moon in this decade and do the other things — not because they are easy, but because they are hard. Because that goal will serve to organise and measure the best of our abilities and skills, because that challenge is one that we are willing to accept, one we are unwilling to postpone, and one which we intend to win."

While terrible leadership sounds like this: "Do you want to go to the moon or not? Then get on with it — NOW! Or I'll give you a rocket that you won't forget!"

So, ask not what the terrible leader can do for you. Ask what you can learn from *The Terrible Leader.*

Jeremy Kourdi, former Senior Vice President,
The Economist Group, and business writer

DAN WHITE
THE TERRIBLE LEADER

 **Marshall Cavendish**
Business

Cover design: Opal Works Co. Limited
Photograph on p312 courtesy of Elle Fallon Photography

Published in 2011 by Marshall Cavendish Business
An imprint of Marshall Cavendish International

PO Box 65829, London EC1P 1NY, United Kingdom
info@marshallcavendish.co.uk

and

1 New Industrial Road, Singapore 536196
genrefsales@sg.marshallcavendish.com
www.marshallcavendish.com/genref

Other Marshall Cavendish offices:
Marshall Cavendish Corporation. 99 White Plains Road, Tarrytown NY 10591-9001,
USA • Marshall Cavendish International (Thailand) Co Ltd. 253 Asoke, 12th Flr,
Sukhumvit 21 Road, Klongtoey Nua, Wattana, Bangkok 10110, Thailand • Marshall
Cavendish (Malaysia) Sdn Bhd. Times Subang, Lot 46, Subang Hi-Tech Industrial Park,
Batu Tiga, 40000 Shah Alam, Selangor Darul Ehsan, Malaysia

Marshall Cavendish is a trademark of Times Publishing Limited

The right of Dan White to be identified as the author of this work has been asserted by
him in accordance with the Copyright, Designs and Patents Act 1988.

A CIP record for this book is available from the British Library

ISBN 978-981-4328-10-4

Printed and bound in Great Britain by
TJ International Limited, Padstow, Cornwall

CONTENTS

ACKNOWLEDGEMENTS

This book is for...

...the thousands of leaders that have passed through my leadership 'classroom'. You are all so different, so special and doing such a good and important job. You inspire me every day.

...all the wonderful people who have shown me, by leading me, what leadership looks like. You have been excellent teachers.

...my wife Claire who patiently listened to every chapter as it was written and re-written. Without you none of this would be worth doing.

...my daughter Leah. Who arrived a few weeks before we went to print. You now have my undivided attention.

Thank you. All of you.

INTRODUCTION

This book is for anyone who has been on a management or leadership training session and thought, "Seriously, this is a load of horse shit". It is for anyone who has tried reading 'leadership literature' and found it to be a little too earnest, a little too trying. It is for anyone who goes to work in the morning, looks around them and wants to shout out, "Why am I surrounded by idiots!?"

Most, if not all, leadership books will give you lots of sound advice on how to become a better leader. This seems reasonable. But here's my problem: are you really going to do things differently, are you really going to 'change your behaviour' because a book tells you to? You've never even met me. I might be some insane bloke living in a block of flats (Americans — read 'apartments') who only goes out for a newspaper once each month in his dressing gown and has seven cats with whom he shares his food and bed...

I'm not, by the way. I don't own a cat or a dressing gown. But still, who does things differently, I mean *really* differently, because a book tells them to? Ok, take out the Torah, the Koran, the Bible etc. and perhaps Mrs. Beaton's cookery books, but after that... So, if you're looking for a book with nicely, neatly parcelled up pieces of advice on how to be a better leader then

pick up a different book. This is going to actually make you
think, not puke. It will make you think about the challenges you
face as a leader. Have a think right now. What makes leadership
tough for you today?

Here's the thing: I've worked in leadership development for
many long years now and leaders really only ever ask me one
thing. Are you ready — this is BIG ok, you're on paragraph four
of the cheapest leadership bible you are ever likely to read and
I'm going straight to the heart of it...

So pay attention...

What they ask is this: *"What should I do in xxx situation?"*

They don't ask generic questions about how to 'maintain
morale' or 'engage and empower my team'. They don't want to
know how to 'communicate with authenticity' or how to 'build
a high performing team'. They want to know what to do in
the exact situation they are in today. This gives the author of
a book about leadership something of a logistical challenge.
One option was to phone up every prospective reader, get
their situation down onto paper, and write a specific chapter
just for you. Wouldn't that be nice? Your own special chapter
just for you! No it wouldn't be nice stupid, because as soon as
you were through that mess, you wouldn't have anything to get
you through the next one. No. That approach, while noble in
spirit, is ridiculous in application. But let's not fall at the first
hurdle. What most writers now do is set about giving you a
series of models, approaches, tools, best practices blah blah blah
that you can use to help plot your way through some leadership

scenarios. But I know you. I can see inside your mind. I know that you'll be full of good intentions and then go and lead and manage in exactly the same way you were before.

So let's stop pretending and do something different instead. Let's turn this whole 'how to be a great leader' thing on its head and see if we can't come at this from a different perspective...

If you read on you will enter the world of the Terrible leader. The Terrible leader doesn't seek to maintain morale, they seek to squash it. The Terrible leader doesn't earn respect, they demand it. The Terrible leader is interested in power and its abuses, not power and its uses. The world of the Terrible leader is gory, alarming, intriguing and at times (if I do say so myself) funny. You will learn about leadership in a completely different way: instead of learning what to do, you will learn what to absolutely avoid. The Terrible leader is a weather vane of the disreputable. Just *don't* do what the Terrible leader would do and you have made a good start. There is another way to learn about leadership through this book (this is a big hint — re-read this bit or you'll miss out): try reversing what the Terrible leader does. The Terrible leader is allowed, indeed they are actively encouraged, to do the very worst thing imaginable.

Question: *What's the opposite of the very worst thing you can do?* Right — it might actually give you an insight into the best course of action.

So, here's the recipe for learning from this book:

1. Get into xxx situation (you know, the one all those leaders ask me about what to do once they're in it), with as little

forethought or planning as you like.

2. Think about what the Terrible leader would do.
3. Do exactly the reverse.
4. Feel confident, have a coffee.

Right, got that? Get into the shit, think Terrible, reverse it, coffee. Your leadership life is about to get so much better.

Because here's the thing: leadership, once you've got into it, and life are inextricably linked. I've spent the last decade working with leaders in Japan, China, Singapore, India, Saudi Arabia, the UAE, South Africa, Switzerland, France, Mexico, the US and Canada to name but a few. The attendees at the programmes I have run have come from at least 40 countries. Apart from earning a lot of airmiles and learning to sleep in the most unpromising of circumstances, I have also found something to be true (second BIG revelation coming up — wakey wakey...): Becoming a leader asks you to change.

And by change I don't mean come into the office earlier and leave later. I don't mean getting all serious during the bonus round. I don't mean say more at team meetings. I mean really *change*. I mean to change who you are. As I write this, my (to be) first-born daughter is still two months from birth, a furiously wriggling bump, who, judging by the level of wriggling, is in the process of sharpening up her cage-fighting skills. Good girl. Now, I don't know this yet exactly, but I suspect the arrival of a first child also demands you to change in a similar way to the advent of leadership responsibility in your life. The difference being the arrival of a first child is rather more sudden and definite. One day it's just there and you learn to deal with it and it's incredibly difficult. Leadership creeps up on you...

The slow, insidious onset of leadership responsibility is matched by a slightly slower and more painful onset of leadership capability. We always seem to lag behind what is required of us as leaders. When you have a baby for the first time everyone says, "It will change your life". They say this over and over and over again, on the assumption presumably that sheer volume of repetition will in some way help you to prepare. But no one sits you down and says the same when you're given your first team leader or shift coordinator role at the age of 23. A wise old crone with a glint in her eye doesn't shuffle over and whisper oblique truisms. No one places a fatherly hand on your shoulder to guide you through the uncertainty and *absolutely* no one gives you the slightest inkling or warning as to the significance of the road onto which you are about to tread.

Let me explain. When you take on the mantle of leadership you take responsibility for one of the most important things on this mortal coil: the well-being, happiness, motivation and morale of your fellow human beings. Humans need more than water, air, food and shelter to live. We need meaning in our lives. We can cope with almost anything provided we have a sense of meaning and purpose in our lives. One view of human beings is that we are essentially greedy and selfish and that we are motivated to do things based upon expected rewards. I believe leaders are here to help elevate us to be so much more than this rather depressing take on humanity. If you lead others, you are here to focus us on the bigger prize, to look at what more we can achieve, to expand our horizons etc. Failure in your responsibility to do this and we will revert to little better than self-focused, grubbing, fearful, insecure animals.

We spend so much time in the workplace in the course of our lifetimes. Your role as leader is all that stands between two positions:

- **Position 1**: work is essentially draining and dull, something to be endured in order to extract sufficient cash from wider society to fulfil my and my family's needs.

- **Position 2**: work is an intrinsically enriching, fulfilling place where I am glad to be able to contribute to something I believe in.

All the research shows that people join organisations but leave managers. You are the person responsible for determining whether the people you lead adopt position 1 or 2. Lives endured or lives fulfilled? With the possible exception of bringing new life into this world, there is no more important responsibility on the planet. You give life meaning. You are a meaning maker. This is serious.

And because this is serious you're going to need to change who you are. Not just a little. A lot. And no one pulls you to one side and explains this deal. No one will explain that with the monetary reward comes a significant increase in expectation. For some it feels natural and straightforward. For others the journey is a struggle you never fully master until the day you retire, leaving the building still scratching your head with a slightly bemused look on your face. Because instead of worrying about what it is you are supposed to do, you are now entering a world of worrying about how others do it and why they are doing it in the first place. You are entering a world where you will need to create the future for people before you even fully know what it will look like, and then excite those people about the idea of reaching that future when maybe it will never work out that way. You will enter a world of paradoxes. You will need to encourage everyone to innovate and yet act consistently. You will need to find ways of saving money while at the same time creating best in class products/experiences etc. You will need to create a sense of identity for your team while at the same time preventing it working in a silo without reference to other teams. In short, you are going to become a tightrope walker. At worst, it's a long way down and there may or may not be a safety net. At best, it is scary and you always seem to be off balance one way or the other. But it can be a wonderful thrill...

So, you won't become a great leader simply by turning up and trying harder or by becoming a more focused version of the original you. You will need to be prepared to examine fundamentally who you are, what you are here to do and how you interact with your fellow human beings on this planet of ours.

This book is deliberately light. It is designed to make you think, not to give you a series of answers that may or may not help given the very specific circumstances you find yourself in.

But just because it is light do not mistake the topic for one that is lightweight. There is no greater, more uplifting, more heroic task than to provide meaningful leadership in the lives of others. This one little book is going to get nowhere near helping you to become a fully functioning leader. You will spend the rest of your life figuring out how to do that. This book is designed to do just one thing — to encourage you to think and reflect, just a little, about how you lead. The great leaders in my experience have just one thing that stands them apart from the others. They see *the leadership itself* as the great challenge, the great conundrum, the great puzzle. The sales, the merger, the project; these are just the scenarios on which to sharpen the skill. Seeing this truth for what it is allows these great leaders to insert the *pause*. The pause between stimulus and response. The pause between something happening and them doing something about it. This is the magic pause that allows them to do something so wonderful, so enlightened, so beautiful that it sends a shiver down my spine every time I see someone do it. The pause allows them to think and then *choose* what to do. They don't just respond like the person they were born to be would naturally respond. They check that knee-jerk response against a couple of alternatives, weigh up in the blink of an eye which response is the best to use right now and then... they change the course of history.

So, this book is designed to do just that one thing, to begin to help you insert that thoughtful pause. With the power of this pause you can become anything you want, because with pause comes choice, and with choice comes control. You won't be able to control what happens around you all the time (some of it you will), but you will be able to control your response to those things, and that is as close to control as we can ever really hope for. If you read this book and pause just once to think about what you could do next as a result of thinking about what the Terrible leader would do, then it will have been more than worthwhile having read this book. So what can you expect if you read this? Perhaps I can most easily illustrate this with an example.

In Chapter 8 we will look at the Terrible approach to motivation. Rather than look at how to motivate people the Terrible leader seeks to squash motivation as a dangerous precursor to independent thought and therefore a threat to your leadership position. So, the Terrible leader works out the different motivational needs of their team (something you *should* also do) in order to work out how best to demotivate them (something you *shouldn't*). For example, the Terrible leader identifies those in their team who are intrinsically goal-oriented and makes sure their targets are ambiguous and unclear. They identify those with a high need for inclusion and force them to work on their own. Your true task is to take these Terrible lessons and switch them on their head. The goal-oriented person needs you to provide clarity, and those with high inclusion needs will require you to involve them. If you get lost in terms of what should work and what really shouldn't don't worry, there's a summary at the back of the book.

So, what follows is I believe what could be best termed an

'anti-leadership' book. This asks, "How bad could you be?" rather than, "What should you do?" Hopefully, you'll have some fun looking at the dark side of leadership and, in some mysterious way, you might learn a few things about the good side along the way. This book is daft. Don't think for a moment I think you're daft too. You will need to pay attention in order to identify the lessons of the Terrible leader, examine them, play around with them and then apply them (if you like) in your own lives.

So, have fun in there. And, errr, don't take it all too seriously...

For good or for bad,
leadership is not about
what you can do.
It is about who you
can become.

part one
Welcome
aboard

At the start of each part of this book we will take stock and reflect on the previous part's chapters. We will use this pause to disengage momentarily from the grubby, disreputable world of the Terrible leader and think for a moment about what lessons, thoughts and ideas we can extract from the previous few chapters.

Learning is a funny old thing, and I believe it is best achieved when you are having a chuckle, with a bit of a smile on your lips and a mind open to the possibilities that new ideas bring. That's why for the vast majority of this book you will notice that the voice of the Terrible leader is pre-eminent. This is my non-serious, tyrannical voice. All of the chapters are written in this voice, and it is meant to be fun rather than instructional. The introductions to the Parts are written as the real me, i.e. the me that doesn't instruct you to turn your people into depressed, stressed and thoroughly downtrodden minions. These parts are your cue to stop and think for a moment about what you just read and what that might mean for you.

So, if you're ready let's get underway. Please remove your safety harness and try to wear as many sharp objects as possible. Before takeoff ensure your tray table is torn from its hinges and thrown yobbishly across the cabin. Keep your mobile phone on and if the stewardess gives you any trouble, kick her in the shins...

CHAPTER I
RECLAIMING TERRIBLE

In 1569, the Tsar of Russia got wind of a plot against him emanating in the cold North West of his realm in the second Russian city of Novgorod. While historians disagree as to the exact nature of this plot (some say they were plotting to replace the Tsar with his relative the Prince Vladimir Staritskii, others that the Novgorodians were plotting to open the city gates to the Poles), what is absolutely clear is that the Tsar took firm and positive action. Andrei Pavlov and Maureen Perrie in their authoritative profile of the event[1] give a very scholarly and dispassionate account of what took place. Being academics, they have tried as hard as possible to give an unemotional and rational account of what the Tsar did to put down this scheme.

> *"On Monday 9th January (1570) the trials began in the Tsar's camp at Gorodishche. The investigation involved appalling methods of torture, with which the oprichnina judges extracted the evidence they required from the accused. The victims were set alight with a mixture of inflammable substances, tied to sledges and taken to the Volkhov, where they were thrust alive under the ice. It was not only adult men who were put to death in this way, but also their wives and their children."*

Welcome to the world of Ivan the Terrible. It doesn't matter how scholarly and rational you set out to be; when it comes to Ivan it just doesn't read well by modern standards. I mean, can you imagine how many employment tribunals he'd be up against today for putting employees' children to death by drowning in a frozen river?

So he wasn't called 'the Terrible' for nothing. But in fact he wasn't called Ivan the Terrible at all, he was called Ivan Groznyi, which translates probably more accurately to 'the Formidable', or 'Dread'. The word *terrible* in English can be interpreted in two ways. More commonly it is something you're not good at; in my case I am terrible at tennis and project planning. Alternatively *terrible* can relate to a terrible punishment or side effect, i.e. the effect to *terrify*. Ivan certainly falls into the latter category: somewhere between one in twelve and one in five of the inhabitants of Novgorod were killed within a few months, not because they'd done anything wrong, but because Ivan was sure they were '*up to something*'. The nature and scale of his oppression is staggering! But how should we interpret Ivan's actions today? Insane? Harsh? Sadistic? Perhaps all of those, but more than any of those he was phenomenally effective.

For example: Ivan's rule lasted for 47 years in the 16th Century from 1533 to 1584, during which time Russia grew at an average rate of 130 square kilometres every day. I don't care if you were your company's top salesman for three years running, what awards you have won, what accolades have been bestowed, you can tear that all up and grow yourself a new definition of 'effective'. To expand your country by 130 square kilometres every day for 47 years you must be doing something right.

So this is our definition of Terrible. Ivan was a model of effectiveness and efficiency. He knew how to control, influence, motivate and achieve seemingly impossible outcomes. He wasn't fluffy or wishy-washy or non-committal. Quite the opposite; he was decisive and firm. In this book, we are going to look at how to become a Terrible leader, and to do that we need a Terrible role model. So from here on, re-tune your internal understanding of the term terrible. 'Terrible' is a desirable epithet, a badge of honour, and something only achieved by the very few greats of leadership.

> 'Terrible' is a desirable epithet, a badge of honour, and something only achieved by the very few greats of leadership.

In this one example, stretching out from Novgorod from 500 years ago, Ivan teaches us so much. Do you ever suspect your people are talking about you behind your back? Ever sniffed a lack of total respect? Of course you have, it happens to all of us. But what did you do about it? Did you:

- Take everyone out for a drink after work to try and make everyone your friend?
- Try and ignore it, it's probably nothing?
- Cosy up to one or two people that you trust to try and find out what's going on?

If you did any of those then shame on you. Ivan would have killed half of them and had the rest of them on the sort of overtime regime that would make your eyes bleed. And would he have confirmed his suspicions with a bit of clever detective work? Of course not! You're the boss, you were given the role because of your superior intuitive skills. So act like you're actually in the role and use those skills! Act on your hunch.

Notice too that, as well as acting on his hunch, Ivan was very careful to extract the necessary 'evidence' he needed in order to justify his actions. Now, we might argue that, when covered with various inflammable substances and set alight, we might not all be the most reliable sources. To be honest, I think we'd all be happy to say anything we needed to in order to get to a bucket of water. But that's not the point. History is written by the winners, and Ivan made sure the right things passed into the record books. Take a leaf from Ivan's book. If you're dealing with a staff member who is always late and you want to sack them, do you keep a careful track record of the subsequent lateness? Would Ivan? Of course not, he'd simply rustle something up that made it looked like the guy had actually never even come to work and gone with that.

Finally, Ivan made it stick. He didn't just punish who he thought were the ring leaders. He went on to punish anyone who had ever had anything to do with them. If you've got a malcontent in your team, do you turf them out? Yes of course, and if you professionally discredit them in the process then bonus points to you, but don't, whatever you do, stop there. Look at the people around that malcontent. Had any of them offered a sympathetic ear? If so, they too could be contaminated, so get rid of them too. Now look a little wider again. You're looking for the wives and children now, the innocents. Get rid of a couple of those too just to drive the point home, i.e. don't just make it dangerous to plot against you, make it so dangerous for there to even be a plot that any plotting or plotters will get squashed by the team itself. Machiavelli said, "*It is safer to be feared than to be loved.*" Ivan reminds us that if you're setting out to be feared, make sure you do it properly!

Ivan achieved a great deal. He helped build an only recently defunct super-power, was a forefather of one of the world's great nations, expanded an empire and brought unity to a previously divided realm. His style as a leader was completely at odds with the existing gentry, who governed through money, heredity and corruption. Ivan governed with a sheer iron force of will, determination and cunning. He was usually prepared to go further and do more than his opponents were. He dared to lead. In our modern world we need Terrible leaders once again. We have fallen into an apathy of 'soft' leadership, coddled by warm words and encouragement that being a good person will necessarily make you a good leader. Well I'm afraid Ivan would know what to say to that. Good but soft people will get chewed up and spat out by the Terrible people every time. The one point these soft teachings make that Ivan would agree with is the importance of authenticity. Today we are told that it is important to be an authentic leader, i.e. a good leader to the core. We are told that it's important that our actions reflect our beliefs and that the leader we are in the work place is aligned to the real person we are at home. Well, in the same way, Ivan was Terrible to the core. He didn't just exterminate mercilessly at work and then come home and be all 'peace and light' with the kids. Far from it; in an argument with his heavily-pregnant daughter, he beat her, making her miscarry. His son, who felt this behaviour to be unacceptable, confronted his father. This, with hindsight, was an error. Ivan hit his son with his walking cane across the head and killed him.

> We have fallen into an apathy of 'soft' leadership, coddled by warm words and encouragement that being a good person will necessarily make you a good leader.

But more on this soft leadership approach. Beware, the *Sissies* are out there, and so are their teachings. We will use the term Sissy for the opposite to Terrible. Sissy leaders are well intended, earnest, ineffective, slow moving, concerned, caring, and probably even actually *like* their staff. They'll tell you, for example, that to motivate someone you must first understand their inner workings. Ivan would agree up to a point. He would argue that if you offer to show someone their own inner workings through the medium of say, a sliced open abdomen, they will be pretty motivated to do whatever you tell them to. The Sissies will tell you to treat mistakes as a 'learning opportunity'. Again, Ivan would just tweak that ever so slightly to treating mistakes as 'an opportunity to teach someone a lesson'. The Sissy approach and the Terrible approach have a few subtle differences and throughout this book you will hopefully learn to spot them. But for now, let us get to know our enemy with a quick field guide to the Sissy leader:

- Places head to one side when listening to you with a studied expression.
- Nods affirmatively when you are talking (they are trying to show that they are listening and they care).
- Asks childish, talk-show-style questions like, "How does that make you feel?"
- Is easily offended by crude jokes or swearing.
- Calls physical violence 'unacceptable'.
- Calls staff by their first name, or possibly even nicknames.
- Has pictures of their family in their office.
- Is quick to praise, even when nothing very special has been achieved.
- Wants to talk about holidays.

If the person sitting opposite you exhibits even some of these traits, you are probably dealing with a Sissy leader. These poor misguided souls have unfortunately misinterpreted leadership as a popularity contest. It probably really matters to them that their staff like them. I know! It's crazy, but don't try and put them right, remember it's not your job to point out the weaknesses of others; it's your job to identify their weaknesses and then work out how to exploit them. For example, when you want to get rid of some really useless people and for reasons best known to the idiots in HR you can't just fire them, these Sissy leaders make great places to offload your morons. Obviously, you don't tell the Sissy that they're morons, you tell them it's a development opportunity. No, don't put the Sissies right, remember, Sissies never make it to CEO, and one more Sissy who turns Terrible is just one more competitor for you.

> It's not your job to point out the weaknesses of others; it's your job to identify their weaknesses and then work out how to exploit them.

Unless you are already advanced in the arts of Terribleness, it is to be expected that from time to time as you read this book, you may inwardly recoil from some of the advice provided. Don't worry. This is just your inner Sissy trying to make itself heard. Inside, we all have an inner Sissy. It is located just behind the knee. If you don't believe me, try creeping up on someone and pushing them behind the knees. They will cave in and fall over backwards, just like Sissy leaders do when asked for pay rises or project deadline extensions. If having read this book you still find yourself behaving in Sissy ways, you might want to consider Sissy-removal-surgery. Similarly, we all have a reservoir of internal Terribleness, located near the spleen which, as we all know, is somewhere near our heart. Or stomach. But definitely not in our legs. The aim of the Terrible leader is to nurture our internal pool of Terribleness and minimise our Sissy. This takes time and hard work (see Chapter 5 — Towards Terrible Day by Day), but is ultimately rewarding both financially and spiritually. Just think of how much money you will make AND how many spirits you will have crushed!

So, each time your inner Sissy calls out — SLAP IT DOWN. You all know that leadership is not a popularity contest. Therefore, logically, it must be an *unpopularity* contest. Would you rather be a creeping, over-sensitive, bleary eyed, whining, sweaty Sissy leader or a clean-cut, robust, decisive, held-in-awe, well dressed, slim and attractive Terrible leader? You already know the answer to that question, you were born to lead and born to lead Terribly. People will hear your name and tremble at the knees (that's their internal Sissy quaking at the thought of a confrontation with a *real* leader). They will tidy their desk or even whole buildings at the mere thought of your visiting. Failing project leaders will commit suicide rather than face your wrath. To quicken the pulse of your staff, you need only raise an eyebrow. Half a gesture of your hand will throw secretaries into frenzied bouts of extra photocopying. People more senior than you won't be able to prevent themselves from brushing crumbs from chairs you are about to sit on. And that chair you do sit on will be treated to a certain degree of reverence and care long after you have left the room.

> The aim of the Terrible leader is to nurture our internal pool of Terribleness and minimise our Sissy.

This is the presence. This is the power. This is Terrible.

Go on; try it on for yourself, like a cloak. Stand in front of a mirror and say, "Rise [insert your name] the Terrible." How does it feel? Let the word and all that comes with it wash over you, cleansing you from your inner Sissy. (If you are quite a literal person and are struggling with the imagination required to achieve this, try bathing in the freshly drawn blood of fawns or puppies — it has a similar effect, and will give your cleaner a thing or two to think about.)

I know you. I can see inside you and I know your inner craving for power, for influence, for control. You have never been encouraged to nurture it, so the desire gutters like a candle on a windy night. Sometimes you dream of what it would be like to have total power over the lives of others, to propel others forward and pull them down, to administer the greatest rewards and the greatest punishments on your whim. Never let this flickering candle die in the wind of modern Sissiness, but from this day onwards nurture it, feed it, strengthen it and watch it flourish at first into a steady flame and with time into a white hot fire that will reach out beyond your team, your department and your whole organisation. Take to your Terrible wings, open them and feel their strength – it is time for you to fledge, to take to the air. As your shadow passes over the land beneath, people will run indoors, animals will whimper and lay down, the wind will cease to rustle the leaves and all will be quiet. You have the position, you have the power – now take it.

Enter The Terrible Leader...

---

[1] *Ivan the Terrible: Profiles in Power,* 2003

Chapter One — Lessons in Terrible

- It is safer to be feared than to be loved.
- When punishing people make sure to punish some extra, innocent people, to drive the point home.
- Leadership is not a popularity contest, therefore it must be an *unpopularity* contest.
- Beware Sissiness and Sissy leaders – but *don't* seek to put them right.

Obviously no one wants to be a Terrible leader in the normal sense of the word. We need to re-tune our understanding of 'Terrible'. We should desire it, covet it, crave it. We want to become The Terrible Leader.

CHAPTER 2
MAKING THE CASE FOR
TERRIBLE LEADERSHIP

In the previous chapter, we reclaimed the term 'Terrible'. Terrible becomes something we can aspire to, something impressive, something we want to be. Emotionally, this all makes exceedingly good sense. But the Terrible leader does not let emotion cloud cold hard logic. We must ask ourselves: does being Terrible make sense in the 21st Century? Just because it worked for Ivan in the 1560s doesn't make it a foolproof approach to adopt. History shows us that two key factors need to be in place before Terrible leadership makes really good sense. Let's have a look at each in turn:

1. Uncertainty

Terrible leadership feeds on uncertainty. If there is a high degree of uncertainty, there is almost nothing you can't get away with as a leader. This is because people experience severe discomfort when faced with change. They immediately fear the worst and assume they are about to lose something, something important to them. Worrying about this potential loss is worse than the loss itself; think about the anticipation around tearing off a plaster/band-aid or those few moments at the top of the high board before you jump. A leader who can hasten the change or loss is nearly always considered a good thing. Terrible leaders can extract two useful lessons from this. Firstly the more uncertain the situation, the greater licence you have for Terrible leadership. Almost anything that gives people any degree of certainty, no matter how tough or unfavourable, will not be pushed against too hard. Secondly, it therefore helps if you can maintain a more or less constant state of flux, uncertainty and change. Never let people settle or get used to things. A settled person is much harder to terrorise than a nomad. Looking around us today, we experience a staggering degree of political, economic, social and environmental uncertainty. Terrible leaders will do well in this environment and should remember to do their bit to ensure these conditions are maintained for future generations of Terrible leaders. To all those out there creating the uncertainty: we salute you, and well done by the way, it really is wonderfully uncertain at the moment.

Winston Churchill, the British Prime Minister during the Second World War, gives us a great example of how uncertainty and Terribleness go hand in hand. The Nazis swept through

> The more uncertain the situation, the greater licence you have for Terrible leadership.

Northern Europe so quickly in 1939 that before Britain or France could really get themselves organised the French had fallen and Britain was faced with an imminent assault on their island fortress (you have to go back to 1066 since that was last successfully achieved, so it was a pretty unthinkable state of affairs). The Allies were in deep trouble, but Britain under Churchill still had one ace, the British Navy. At the time the

British navy was almost a super-power in its own right, and even with Britain surrounded and teetering the Germans definitely did not rule the waves. But what about the French navy? A considerable force, this was now technically under German control, holed up in ports around the world under the terms of an Armistice drawn up between France and Germany. Technically, this armistice put the French fleet out of reach of the Germans, and in reality, Hitler did not have the resources to commandeer it, spread around the world as it was. Furthermore, the French Admiral Darlan had given Churchill personal assurances that he would scupper his fleet should the Germans try and take control. Most of the French fleet was distributed around the world but there was a sizeable force at anchor near Oran in Algeria, including four battleships and six destroyers.

In Churchill's shoes, what would you do now? Essentially the situation could play out in four ways:

1. The French fleet could surrender itself to British command;

2. The French fleet could remain peaceably at anchor throughout the war;

3. The French fleet could at any time be surprised by a German force and boarded; or

4. The Germans could try and take the French fleet and the French might successfully or partially successfully scupper their own boats.

The situation was uncertain. The US was still undecided about entering a European war, especially if Britain did not look like it was going to stay the distance. The Germans expected the British to capitulate pretty quickly — things were looking bleak. Against this uncertain backdrop, a Terrible leader stood up and took action. Churchill acted ruthlessly. In early July 1940, he sent an ultimatum to the whole French fleet giving them a number of options:

1. Sail out of port with the British navy and hand the boats over to British command.
2. Sail to French ports in the West Indies beyond the effective reach of the Germans.
3. Sink your ships within six hours.
4. Let us do the sinking for you.

> Against this uncertain backdrop, a Terrible leader stood up and took action. Churchill acted ruthlessly.

The French couldn't believe the last two options were seriously going to be enforced by an ally. Several commanders handed their ships over without a fuss. Some resisted British boarding parties in Portsmouth with a handful of casualties. At Oran, a British naval task force was assembled and delivered the ultimatum to the French fleet at anchor. There was great confusion and the French simply refused to believe that the British would open fire. After six hours, and with negotiations continuing, the British scrambled aircraft from HMS Ark Royal to drop magnetic mines at the mouth of the harbour. The French were now trapped. The British negotiation party left aboard their launches and, once out of range, HMS Hood, the largest battleship on either side, opened fire. Again, the French assumed that this was for show, especially as the shells did not find their mark. The French were at anchor, could not manoeuvre or bring their big guns to bear on the British ships, which thanks to their superior range were out of reach anyway. The mines sealed their exit from port, so the French sat back and waited for negotiations to resume. HMS Hood continued to shell the French fleet, the third salvo finding its mark and hitting the Bretagne, which exploded and went down with 977 crew dead. The unthinkable continued and when the smoke had cleared the French had lost three battleships, three destroyers (the rest escaped through the mines), 1,297 men killed and 350 wounded. The British lost six men and six aircraft.

The British Admiral (Somerville) said at the time that it was, "*The biggest political blunder of modern times and will rouse the whole world against us... we all feel thoroughly ashamed*". Somerville could not have been more wrong as this incident showed the Americans just how determined Churchill was to defeat the Nazis, and shortly afterwards entered the war on the side of the Allies. Churchill exhibited awesome Terribleness in this act. He was ruthless and understood that in the face of uncertainty, the Terrible leader is rarely questioned and often rewarded.

Interestingly, a little over two years later in November 1942, the Germans attempted to take the French fleet anchored at Toulon. As they had always promised to do, the French scuttled and sank anything of any military value long before the Germans could do anything about it...

> In the face of uncertainty, the Terrible leader is rarely questioned and often rewarded.

2. Competition

The second key condition for Terrible leadership lies in competition. In non-competitive situations Terrible leadership often goes unrewarded, and is seen as unnecessary or over-the-top. Obviously we know that Terrible leadership is *always* a good thing, but you don't want to go casting your pearls before swine, as the saying goes. Top sprinters save their fastest times for the most competitive situations, the World Championships or the Olympics. Terrible leaders need to operate in much the same way.

Stalin knew a thing or two about Terrible leadership and competition. Today we may pale somewhat at some of his more ambitious policies, but it is interesting to reflect back and look at how he actually got to power. Between Lenin's stroke in 1922 and his heart attack and death in 1924, it was by no means certain that Stalin would succeed him to head the Communist party. The balance of power swung delicately between Trotksy, Kamenev, Zinoviev and Stalin, with Bukharin the editor of *Pravda* and a leading theorist playing a key role if not quite being a contender for the leadership. Trotsky was the glamorous, well-known, eloquent leader of the Red Army. He was technically second in command to Lenin, the most senior and, on paper, the obvious successor. However, the army was small post-WWI demobilisation, he was relatively isolated and did not have as much real power as Stalin did in his role as head of the Party (Gensek, or General Secretary of the Central Committee). Kamenev and Zinoviev saw the greater threat to their future aspirations coming from the louder Trotsky, so formed a triumvirate with Stalin during Lenin's years of periodic collapse and recovery. Kamenev was the less ambitious, but he held significant influence chairing the Moscow Soviet and being Lenin's deputy in the Sovnarkom, posts he'd held since the end of the First World War. The Sovnarkom was the Council of the People's Commissars, a sort of worker's congress that took care of the administration of Soviet Russia. Ultimately, decrees passed in the Sovnarkom had to be ratified at the Soviet Congress, but they routinely were and it was therefore a powerful bloc in the race to the leadership. Zinoviev was the head of Comintern (The Communist International organisation aimed at bringing communism to the world) and also held significant influence. The scene was set for a lengthy and protracted struggle.

Now, a Sissy leader faced with this situation might concentrate on doing everything they could to strengthen their position. They might form alliances and work extra hard and extra diligently to deliver results. They might do more to understand the needs of the various players in the situation and find ways of meeting those needs. And Stalin did do some of these things, but Stalin wasn't a Sissy leader. He was willing to do anything to edge his rivals to the top post and he knew a Terrible truism that the others may have known (they had all survived a bloody civil war after all), that it is much easier to make others look bad than it is to make yourself look good. Don't play to win. Play to not lose. He rightly assessed Trotsky as his greatest threat and set out to undermine him. On the basis that an enemy's enemy is a friend, he collaborated with Kamenev and Zinoviev, the three of them presenting themselves as a united front in the face of uncertainty around Lenin's health. Lenin disliked factionalism and Trotsky's supporters were isolated and made to appear divisive. The way Stalin painted it, Trotsky was denying the wishes of a dying hero.

> It is much easier to make others look bad than it is to make yourself look good.

Lenin passed away in 1924 having suffered for years with atherosclerosis. Stalin personally oversaw Lenin's ascension to the mythic post of a Bolshevik Messiah, building him a mausoleum and having him embalmed in ways previously unknown to science so that his body would last indefinitely. He then worked furiously to talk up the disagreements between Trotsky and Lenin, who of course, being dead, did little to put anyone right. A key event at this time was Lenin's funeral, when the Party and the whole country mourned the passing of an iconic and legendary figure. Trotsky did not attend. In 1996 Edvard Radzinsky published his Stalin biography, using as source material previously secret Soviet archives. (If you want to know more about Stalin's Terribleness this is a good place to start.) A telegram from Stalin to Trotsky at the time reveals the reasons behind Trotsky's failure to attend Lenin's funeral:

"Funeral takes place on Saturday, you cannot get there in time. The Politburo thinks that the state of your health makes it essential for you to go to Sukhumi. Stalin."

Trotsky's own health was poor and there was a spa at Sukhumi where it was planned he would take a cure. So perhaps Stalin was just thinking about Trotsky's health? That would be fine if the funeral actually was to take place on the Saturday. But in fact the funeral was scheduled for Sunday and Trotsky's failure to attend was a blot against his name he was never able to clear. From that point on, Trotsky was regularly labelled as an 'oppositionist' by Stalin and his allies, culminating in his banishment in 1928 and eventual murder in Mexico with the famous ice-pick in 1940.

Kamenev and Zinoviev were both shot eventually in 1936 on Stalin's orders on some dreamed up charge of organising a terrorist 'centre' (it was all a ruse by Stalin and during the 1980s they were both cleared of any such involvement). In 1925 the issue facing Stalin was how to remove them both from power. In Bukharin he found his excuse and deployed the same ruse he had worked on Trotsky. Zinoviev and Kamenev both opposed Bukharin's more right-wing stance. Stalin again labelled them as oppositionist and accused them of attempting to splinter the Party. Zinoviev was removed from the leadership of Comintern and Kamenev was packed off as the Ambassador to a foreign country. At the same time, Stalin embraced Bukharin as a Party favourite. Bukharin was not a serious threat to Stalin, but he was the last of the heavy-weights standing from the period when

Stalin had had to fight for his life and the leadership of the Party and he really should have seen the writing on the wall. For the very same right-wing tendencies that Stalin had rallied around and punished Kamenev and Zinoviev for opposing, Bukharin landed up in prison, to be shot at last in 1938. Stalin personally oversaw the records from Bukharin's trial and made sure that what the world believes Bukharin said at the very end suited his version of history.

Stalin went on to mercilessly weed out tens of thousands of political opponents, possible political opponents, old school revolutionaries, unruly army leaders, their wives and acquaintances. Most were shot or banished to forced labour camps (gulags) in the far north. Their numbers were swelled by hundreds of thousands of petty criminals, people who had been overheard telling political jokes and those who had committed the age-old crime of being in the wrong place at the wrong time. It is estimated that over 1.6 million made their way into the gulags to provide the USSR with a huge, very cheap form of physical labour. The numbers arrested were not a reflection of anti-Stalinist feeling in the country but depended on the scale of the civil engineering feats planned. The gulag prisoners were in fact arrested to order. Stalin kept different factions of the communist party at each other's throats and maintained a healthy turnover of opponents so that competition was always alive and well within Stalinist Russia. That same level of tense, histrionic competition served to make sense of his Terribleness and made sure no one questioned him. As late as 1959, six years after his death and long after Stalin's gulags and worse had come to light, Winston Churchill made a speech to the House of Commons saying;

"It was Russia's great good luck that in the years of its greatest tribulations the country had at its head a genius and an unyielding military leader like Stalin."

Stalin didn't just get away with being one of the most ruthless, dictatorial, murderous leaders of all time; he was positively praised for it.

So, as you can see, Terrible leadership flourishes under the right conditions. Look around you now and think about how uncertain or competitive your working environment is. Think about your team, your department, your company, your industry, the economic outlook of your country. Does it look stable and safe or uncertain and competitive? Right! It's uncertain and competitive isn't it?! More so now than it has been for hundreds of years most likely. So Terrible leadership should make sense, which leaves us with an uncomfortable truth: why aren't there more Terrible leaders? There are a lot, don't get me wrong, and even more who are actively trying to unpick their own true, innate Terribleness, but it still seems to me that given these ripe conditions, there should be more Terrible than Sissy leaders out there, not the other way around. There is a very simple reason for why this is so: habituation. We have simply become used to the level of uncertainty and competition that surrounds us. From a young age, we are in open and active competition with our classmates for the best grades, the best places in schools, scholarships, sports prizes and so on. In Japan, the average 15-year-old works for around 14 hours per day. In England, competition for scholarships to good schools drives children to learn two instruments, a language, several sports and to get good grades

> Given these ripe conditions, there should be more Terrible than Sissy leaders out there.

in every subject, all by the age of 11. No wonder then that by adulthood, all round the world, we are accustomed to a level and degree of competition that would make our ancestors suck their teeth. And that's just competition! Never before have we had such a degree of uncertainty about our future. In the 1960s Terrible leaders enjoyed the uncertainty and fear generated by the Cold War to fully express their Terribleness. Today we are so much better connected through the internet and 24-hour news channels that we can all get ourselves into a lather about a true smorgasbord of uncertainty: international terrorism, global warming, peak oil, sustainability, over-population, SARS-style epidemics and financial melt-down, let alone the hideous rise of reality TV. Against that backdrop, it can be quite hard for a Terrible leader to punch through and justify their actions. Let me try and illustrate the point with an example.

I want you to imagine that you live in a small house in the woods, with your two small children (your spouse tragically died several years ago). The house is a nicely appointed, well taken care of home that you have built lovingly over the period of many years. You have many valuable items in the house, being a keen collector of antiques. You hunt in the woods for deer and rabbits which you eat, so you have guns too. Now, one morning, you hear shouting. Looking outside, you see someone approaching through the branches. It is a large man making a lot of noise, and he sounds quite threatening, although indistinct at this point. So you go to your gun locker and take down your shot-gun, step outside the front door and... taking careful aim, blast him away. Seem unreasonable?

> **Context A:** The house is in a wood in the middle of the Canadian wilderness in the 1870s. No one has approached your house for over three years. You have heard of a group of desperadoes raiding houses and taking away anything they can use, killing people as they go. The act now seems pretty reasonable.

> **Context B:** The house is in a small wood just outside a small European village in the 2000s. A well known walking trail goes past the house and you typically see twenty or thirty people walking past the house every day. Now the act looks pretty odd.

We live today in a Context B world. Terrible acts look worse because people have become habituated to both uncertainty and competition. There are two critical lessons that the Terrible leader needs to extract from this fact. Firstly, get used to the idea that sometimes your deeds as a truly Terrible leader will not always be met with popular acclaim — but, and here's the important bit, it doesn't make them any less effective. Whether shocking or otherwise, Terrible deeds of leadership are the effective ones, not the Sissy ones. Think back to our crash course on Terrible in the face of uncertainty from Churchill. Early in the war, it seemed quite an alarming course of action, but far worse was done later in the war (think about Dresden) with less alarm because people had become so used to a much higher background level of uncertainty and competition.

Our second key learning point is this: if the background level of uncertainty and competition is high, Terrible deeds, despite their appropriateness, might stand out in the eyes of a habituated populace. Terrible leaders will do well

> Your deeds as a truly Terrible leader will not always be met with popular acclaim — but, and here's the important bit, it doesn't make them any less effective.

therefore to further increase those very conditions of uncertainty and competition so that people are once again acutely aware of them, making those same Terrible deeds that previously stood out melt into the background. So, don't whinge about the situation you find yourself in today, change it. Make the conditions ripe for you to deliver your fully-honed Terribleness that you will acquire if you practice the teachings from this book. But how to create uncertainty and competition artificially? Here are some practical steps you can take to keep your working environment in a constant state of flux and competitive stress...

Uncertainty — maintaining the shades of grey

To maintain a healthy level of uncertainty around you and your team try:

- Telling slightly different things to different members of the team; make sure that in the details they are able to read some potentially big changes afoot. For example, "Well, it might not be that *you* need to do that in the future..." or, "...of course, if that department even exists then...". Keep drip feeding these kinds of comments into everyday conversations.

- Changing your mind routinely and regularly; don't do this too quickly either, ideally you need to let people get halfway to implementing your initial directive, making promises to their teams or customers before you change your mind. This helps to keep people on their toes and, if done regularly enough, will flush out any potential rivals for your role when they complain. It helps if at least once a year you actually let someone get all the way to completion on a major project before shelving it. Try and rotate this practice so that everyone in the team gets a dose of this once a year.

- Changing reporting lines regularly; don't let people settle into routines of reporting lines. True Terrible leaders also use the marvellous technique of reversing reporting lines occasionally. A truly first-class Terrible practice, this ends up with managers reporting to the people they previously managed. Nothing serves better to dampen an individual's resolve, self-belief and confidence than reporting to someone who they have previously been in charge of. Be careful to make these changes quite rapidly to get the full value from them. If that sort of change happens over many months or even years, it rather loses its effect. Aim to make the change in a number of weeks to really get the full benefit.

- Keeping people guessing; be careful about divulging too much about what you know about the future of the team or organisation. The knowledge you gain from above, from those more senior than you, is a privilege and needs to be carefully guarded. This knowledge acts as the 'rules of the game' and allows you to position yourself to be the best effect. Don't give other people that advantage, they will use it to overhaul you if you are not careful.

- Changing the goalposts; people derive certainty from clear goals. When a person scores a goal in football, we know (in 99.9% of times and not including the debacle of England vs. Germany in the 2010 World Cup) whether the goal was in or not, and you can see the satisfaction the player gains from having scored a goal, what with all that unsightly kissing and hugging that goes on. Imagine the game being played in total darkness, with no way of knowing whether or not shots were going in or even close to the goal. The result would be declared at the end and no one would be any the wiser as to who had scored the winning goal – you can just make that bit up. That would put an end to all that unsightly celebration. It would also make the players much easier to manage, and far less expensive, as you could easily prevent any one player from believing they were any more talented or valuable than any other. You have created a level playing field! It is the same in the world of work. Try to avoid giving people clarity about their goals and targets. This prevents them from connecting their everyday actions with successful outcomes, and in turn prevents them from becoming unmanageably confident or over-bearing. Just watch as your Sissy colleagues get request after request for pay rises or promotions from their people! No such problems for the Terrible leader; your people will just feel lucky they have a job at all.

Competition — divide and rule

We are so used to competition in the workplace it helps if you can dial it up a notch or two. Try some of the following:

- When a senior member of your team moves on, or you get rid of them because they were useless, rather than appoint a direct replacement, give the job to two more junior members of the team. This is cheaper (you can avoid pay rises) and it means they'll fight it out trying to win your approval in the belief you are looking for one of them to 'emerge' as the obvious candidate.

- If you are lucky enough to manage whole teams of minions, it helps if you can set them up to have somewhat overlapping responsibilities. Don't make the situation too clear. If you do, the teams are likely to become cocky and confident, and this is exactly the breeding ground for rivals you want to avoid creating. Think about finance and administration for example... The opportunities for overlap are endless. Good overlap means plenty of abrasive, rubbing edges in your organisation. You can then swoop in and be the all-knowing super-leader who arbitrates. Nothing moves without you being called in, your power is unassailable. These overlaps not only create competition, but also uncertainty — so this really is a good way of creating the right conditions for Terrible leadership.

- Give the same project to two different teams or people. This is a very open way of creating competition, and as such should be used with caution. Far better to create competition without the Sissies and HR-types being able to pin it on you. However, sometimes, when you think you can get away with it, it can be a good idea to simply get people doubled up on important projects. It will irritate the hell out of the people assigned to the project when they work out they have a competitor, and you will have to intervene at this point to avoid any risk of their collaborating in the future. But if the project is important, and your good name is resting on the result, two heads are better than one. You can always fire the less successful project manager later on when the project is successfully delivered and you have taken the credit.

- A more subtle way to divide and conquer is to divide people's loyalties. You will all have seen the following situation arise at work. Two highly capable people working together, sitting close to one another and becoming close friends, let's call them Mr. Kourdi and Mr. Liu. The amount of work they actually do dwindles as they spend more and more time chatting and joking around. Now, obviously, you would normally just fire them both and make an example of them for being slackers, but if HR won't let you because of some arcane directive or other, try this out instead. Have Mr. Kourdi report to Mr. Liu and put Liu under a lot of pressure to get more from Kourdi. That will make their heads swivel! Liu will want to try and demonstrate to Kourdi that his promotion will do nothing to dent their friendship. Kourdi, quite rightly, won't believe this for a moment. Liu will also be keen to impress you that you were right to make your decision. It helps if you can fill Liu's head with how much you have always rated him over Kourdi and how much you need them to really improve their overall output, suggesting it is Kourdi that is the source of the problem.

We have looked at two critical conditions for the full expression of Terribleness: uncertainty and competition. Thankfully, the 21st Century is almost subtitled 'the competitive and uncertain century' so we can feel confident that taking a

Terrible approach will be well rewarded, effective and sensible. Paradoxically, our challenge in the 21st Century is that we already have these conditions in abundance as a constant background to our everyday lives, and therefore as Terrible leaders it is our responsibility to dial up our people's experience of uncertainty and competition, thus making our Terrible leadership not only appropriate but also palatable.

> As Terrible leaders, it is our responsibility to dial up our people's experience of uncertainty and competition.

George Bush Jnr. had the right idea. He wanted to invade Iraq, and what business is it of ours to question his motives. The guy had a lot of ordnance, and in the world of Terrible leadership, might is right. Now, the clever bit was how to make it seem like a good idea to everyone else. As aspiring Terrible leaders, we appreciate that what George Junior was doing was making an example of the people of Iraq. The message was clear. *"If anyone else tries flying planes into our big shiny buildings we're going to go out there and kill more innocent people than you would even think possible"*. The message is just the same as Ivan's in the previous chapter, basically don't even think about plotting against the United States. George was quite right, it doesn't matter who you kill, or even if they are the right people (in fact, it's probably better if they are the wrong people like the women and children Ivan killed in the previous chapter), it only matters that you kill lots and you kill fast, and boy did he do a good job. The medical Journal, *The Lancet*, estimates that in the 18 months after the invasion, around 100,000 Iraqi civilians died as a direct result of the war or the resulting breakdown in civil security. By June 2006 this figure may have grown to as high as 600,000. The Americans, meanwhile, have lost in the region of 5,000, mostly military personnel. Iraq became an incredibly dangerous place to live for everyone there and is generally considered the most dangerous place on the planet. Now, the really clever bit was getting people behind him, and to do that he used a good old dose of uncertainty. The argument basically goes:

- There are terrorists out there (true).
- They will strike again (probably true — but excellent uncertainty here).
- They are either in Iraq (probably not true) or supported by the Iraqi government (plausible, unproven).
- The Iraqi government has plans to attack its neighbours and our allies (not true).
- And they have weapons of mass destruction to do it with, ready to go in like, less than an hour (not true).

Just enough truth, plenty of big fat lies and a big old dollop of old-fashioned uncertainty and suddenly a war seems like a pretty good idea. Way to go George! George Bush Jnr. cannot exactly be listed as a role model Terrible leader. He manages to combine, at least in elements, both meanings of the word *Terrible*. He also had a good dose of the Sissy about him too, but we can certainly hold this example up as truly outstanding. At the time of the invasion, the US was ranked the No.1 military power in the world. Iraq was ranked 37th. The US have around 18,000 military aircraft, Iraq had 651. The US have around 30,000 tanks, Iraq had 2,580. David stood a better chance against Goliath. This was more like David vs. Goliath plus all of Goliath's friends and family. And yet, despite that, the Bush administration actually managed to get other powerful countries to *help*! And the Bush administration didn't stop there, they used the uncertainty and fear generated by 9/11 to push through many more Terrible acts of leadership. 9/11 was a terrible, terrible event, but quite rightly the Bush administration responded positively to the new situation it found itself in. Governments around the world followed this good example, using the new uncertainty to push through all sorts of laws aimed at curtailing individual rights and moving power to governments. Good work!

In this chapter, we have made the case for Terrible leadership. We have tried to illustrate that while Terrible leadership might not be appropriate or even wise all of the time, it certainly is now. If you need more convincing, consider this simple situation, one I am sure you have been in plenty of times. You are with a large group at work, say more than 10 people, and you have to make a decision about what to do next in a major critical project. It is pretty obvious what needs to be done, and yet somehow the decision takes hours, and in the end, the decision made is unfocused, unclear and over-

> While Terrible leadership might not be appropriate or even wise all of the time, it certainly is now.

complicated. We have all been there, it happens all the time. What we are looking at here is the logic of the least decision makers. Sissy leaders talk about involving and engaging people, getting people to contribute to the decisions that affect them and listening to their points of view. This kind of puke-inducing behaviour, while not only wrong, is also dangerous. Once again, remember, you were promoted into the leadership role, not your team members. And why were you promoted and not them? Because they are idiots. It is very simple. Your judgement, your thinking and your decisions are necessarily better than those of the people that report to you, precisely because they report to you! It is very dangerous to open up debate and decision making to your team, it is even more dangerous to listen to the people in your team. You were promoted and paid to make the decisions, so stop acting like the Sissy, man-up and make them!

> And why were you promoted and not them? Because they are idiots. It is very simple.

Chapter Two — Lessons in Terrible

- Uncertainty and competition are the key ingredients for ensuring the appropriateness of Terrible leadership.
- The 21st Century is replete with uncertainty and competition, and as a result, most people have become habituated to these conditions.
- It is therefore the job of the Terrible leader to increase the levels of uncertainty and competition so that our Terribleness (appropriate, but sometimes unpalatable) is found to be more acceptable.
- You can increase uncertainty by maintaining shades of grey in the organisation — try and prevent people achieving clarity about what it is they should do.
- You can increase competition by setting up internal rivalries between individuals and teams — by dividing, by keeping people clawing at each other rather than us, we conquer.

Remember — Terrible leadership only makes sense under certain conditions. We are completely surrounded by these conditions, indeed we are drowning in them. Now is the time for Terrible.

CHAPTER 3
LESSONS FROM HISTORY

History is littered with marvellous examples of Terrible leaders. The list is long and we should salivate at the chance to learn from the likes of Caligula, Genghis Khan, Vlad the Impaler, Ivan the Terrible, Stalin and many more. Sure, they killed a few people along the way, and in these pages I do not intend to judge, defend or prosecute them for their more maniacal acts. No, instead, we shall sit back, watch and learn from these masters. These leaders really knew a thing or two about strong, decisive leadership. Sissy leaders beware...

We shall take a number of lessons from these historical bastions of Terrible leadership and then examine each in turn within the context of a modern working environment. I want to show you that you can bring a little historical flavour of Terribleness to your everyday working lives. You too can 'do a Vlad' or 'pull an Ivan'...

Lesson 1: Learning from mistakes

Remember those Sissy leaders? They will want you to treat every mistake made by one of your direct reports as 'a learning opportunity'. We have, by now, realised the pure soft-mindedness of this sort of approach. The day you catch yourself treating a mistake as a 'learning opportunity' is the day to check yourself into the old people's home and start some peremptory drooling. This is not the way of the Terrible leader. And that is not to say we ignore mistakes, quite the opposite. Now, let's learn from some leaders who knew how to handle the odd dip in performance from their staff...

Vlad the Impaler, or Vlad Dracula, ruled Wallachia (around a third of modern-day Romania) on and off between 1431 and 1476. He knew a thing or two about Terrible leadership, the clue is in the name, you don't get called 'the Impaler' without having had something of a penchant for the odd random act of Terribleness.

Vlad had a troubled route to the throne. Power in Wallachia switched intermittently between the land-owning gentry and the princes, of which Vlad was among the latter. During his childhood, a revolt proved

> You don't get called 'the Impaler' without having had something of a penchant for the odd random act of Terribleness.

the downfall of his father, Vlad Dracul, and the gentry killed both his father and brother, rather gruesomely by burying them alive. Many years passed, during which Vlad spent a good bit of time in a Turkish prison learning a thing or two about how to really make people squirm. Eventually, Vlad regained the throne. Now, those land-owners who had orchestrated the revolt that resulted in the death of his father and brother turned out to have backed the wrong horse; they made a big mistake. A Sissy leader might have tried to patch things up with the land-owners, to try and heal the wounds of history. Not Vlad. He knew that action was expected one way or the other so he offered an olive branch. He invited all of the most prominent land-owners in the capital city of Wallachia to a big feast in his castle. They were apparently very happy with this turn of events as it looked as though the new Prince was willing to forgive, forget and move on. After all, it had been the better part of 20 years since the death of his father and brother.

Vlad threw a good party too, lots to eat and drink, and the event lasted long into the night. We don't know exactly when or how, but at some point late at night the guests, having eaten and drunk their fill, began to leave. The castle gates were closed, as you would expect at night, so the first leavers set off to find someone to open the gates for them. Soon a crowd of several hundred happy, slightly drunk partygoers formed at the gate house. I should imagine songs were sung, jokes were told and much general hilarity indulged in. As time wore on this mood might have become tinged with a mild apprehension, but it seems unlikely that the townspeople could have had any inkling as to what was about to happen. The gates were not opened, and guards descended on the crowds, escorting them off in small groups to be 'interviewed' by Vlad Dracula. He was particularly interested in those old enough to have been involved in the revolt against, and death of, his family. In the end, it was extremely hard to discern who had and who had not been involved and who was simply around at the time.

Vlad was a pragmatic man, not fazed by this apparent lack

of hard evidence. He simply marched 200 of the guests (this must have been the morning of the day after the party by now) out in front of the castle gates and placed them under heavy guard. Then, with the small remainder of the guests watching, he took each of them in turn and had them driven alive onto a long, pointed stake. This process of impaling was pretty brutal. The stake is driven in through... well, you can imagine where, and then driven through your body. It might, but typically doesn't, kill you outright. Instead, you are left to die as the stake is planted in the ground. It might take you a day or more to actually succumb. The screaming, noise and gore of 200 people being impaled alive must have been horrific. It was said that the earth around the castle ran with blood.

Vlad was subsequently plotted against, but not for a while, and not by these people. They learned a valuable lesson that day — don't mess with Vlad. This was a lesson they would never forget. He worried less about actual guilt than with symbolic action. Not all of the 200 were guilty, but they were all impaled. The question: "Can we plot against our leader and get away with it?" The answer: "Not unless you want a sharpened stake rammed up your fundament."

But Vlad didn't keep his lessons for the well-to-do. Not at all, he was equally prepared to admonish the mistakes of the most grovelling of his underlings. Legend has it that while passing through the city in his carriage, he was detained by traffic or some stoppage. While waiting and gazing out of the

> **Worry less about actual guilt than with symbolic action.**

window, he noticed a peasant walking along with a particularly shabby set of mended, re-stitched clothes. Beckoning to the shoddily dressed peasant to come closer, he asked him who had patched his tunic. "My wife," was the response. "Bring her to me," replied Vlad. The woman was brought in front of Vlad there and then and asked to verify that she had indeed been responsible for the rather slap-dash repair work.

Vlad again has the opportunity to teach a lesson, this time about slovenliness and taking pride in your work. But how to punish someone in this situation — something proportionate, something in line with the crime committed? How about a bit of impaling? The great thing with a soubriquet like 'Impaler' is that it gets you out of any tight spot. Imagine the number of questions and queries you must get from your minions! "What shall we do with the captives? What should we do with the poor people? What should we do about the criminals? We've got some immigrants... We don't know what to do with these travelling merchants. This circus has just arrived in town..." Vlad had a ready reckoner for all these situations and more. And the stake makers must have been kept busy as it is estimated that, at his height, there we upwards of 20,000 impaled bodies in varying states of decay around his castle at Targoviste. Imagine the smell! 20,000 decomposing bodies, ranging from still alive and screaming through to positively putrid. And did people learn from their mistakes under Vlad's rule? Well, you can be certain that peasant woman never sewed sloppily ever again!

Now, let's examine Vlad's lesson in teaching people a lesson within the context of a modern 21st Century organisation. Typically, we communicate via email these days, so what follows is a typical email exchange you may well recognise. Put yourself in the shoes of Vladimir Chapman, the leader in this scenario. He is being alerted to a problem in the production department of the factory he manages...

To: *Vladimir.I.Chapman@vticomponents.com*
From: *Inna.b.Trubble@vticomponents.com*

Subject: Line outage — issue with monitors

Hi Vladimir,
Just wanted to alert you to an issue with the line-upgrade project. As you'll be aware this week we were due to install new monitors on the line to detect and correct line feed errors so that we could reduce the number of line stoppages. We are expecting these monitors to reduce stoppages by 50%, which equates to 2,000 more units processed every week. These new monitors replace old, out-of-date components that we took off the line over the weekend. Unfortunately the new monitors were delivered without the right software and so do not work. The software is on its way and should be with us by the end of the week.

The problem we have is that, having dismantled the old monitors we have accidentally erased their programming and no one knows how to re-programme them. The company that used to make them has gone out of business. It looks like we may have no choice but to manually assemble for the rest of this week until the new monitor software arrives. Manually, we can only assemble 10% of the product compared to the automated line.

I accept full responsibility for this error and am working hard with my team to ensure that as much product is assembled as possible, bringing in temporary workers and working double shifts this week.

My sincere apologies, please do let me know if you have any questions.

Best regards,
Inna Trubble
Production Team Leader
VTI Components
Greater Wallachia

Ok, Inna's made a big mistake, not thinking through the possible implications of taking monitors off-line, and she didn't have a good contingency or back-up plan. This is going to cost the company a lot of money, and, even worse, might affect some of the key metrics that determine your personal bonus. This is intolerable. What would you do?

1. Re-assure Inna that you are sure she is doing everything in her power to bring the situation back under control and that you appreciate her hard work and dedication.

2. Ask what she needs from you to help her reduce the impact of the problem.

3. Offer to come and help out on the assembly line.

4. Ask Inna to conduct a full review as to how this error occurred and schedule time to talk through the situation regarding her own personal development.

5. Ask for a review of change procedures across the whole factory.

If any of the above feels like what you might actually do, then we have still got some work to do to move over from Sissy to Terrible. Don't worry, it's only Chapter 3, there is still plenty of time to rout the inner Sissy! Ask someone to cane you across the back of the knees — this should help some. Now, think back to Vlad's example. What would he do in a situation like this? You've got it, he'd impale her. Now, unless you work in a very forward-thinking part of the world, actual impalement has its logistical challenges. Keeping the necessary sharpened stakes in your office or in an open-plan situation might prove awkward. Generally, extreme forms of physical violence won't do much for your career unless you are being managed by another Terrible leader and you manage to get things done very quietly. Impaling is one of the harder forms of murder to keep quiet incidentally, so no, actual impalement is probably a non-starter. But what is today's equivalent? Consider the following:

Increase the uncertainty and anxiety, perhaps responding with an email after a couple of hours saying something like this:

To: *Inna.b.Trubble@vticomponents.com*
From: *Vladimir.I.Chapman@vticomponents.com*

Subject: Re: Line outage — issue with monitors

Not good...

Vladimir Chapman
General Manager
VTI Components
Greater Wallachia

Leave her hanging for the moment. There is no need to show your hand at this stage, but it helps if you can express your dissatisfaction in a non-committal way. This will alert Inna that you are very unhappy about the situation, it suggests you may take further action, but she has no idea what that might be. You have now created one of our favourite Terrible prerequisites — uncertainty. And all with just two words — you see, Terrible leadership is not only effective, it can also be very quick. Now that you have set the stage, you have a number of options:

1. Get in contact with your superiors explaining the situation. Re-assure them that any dip in production will be made up in coming weeks and express your exasperation and dissatisfaction with Inna and her team. Let your boss know that serious action will be taken and that you will soon have the situation under control. You get one point for this — it's a basic act of Terribleness, but it is important to focus the blame on Inna and those in her area and away from you personally.

2. Schedule a meeting with Inna for later that day, perhaps after most people have gone home, say around 8pm. Keep her waiting till around 8.25pm. Then do a lot of shouting. Does she realise that cock-ups like this are driving the company into the ground? People would lose their jobs if we ran the company like this! She clearly isn't cutting it in the business etc. Remember to really ratchet up the volume and the hand gestures. Perhaps stand up

and talk down to her — that should do the trick. Lots of accusatory body language like pointing is never a bad plan. Now that she is softened up, ask her whose fault it was. You get three points for this kind of behaviour because it potentially generates two new options:

a. If Inna says the situation is her fault and her fault alone, you are left with only one real option and that is to fire her. Immediately is good, tell her to go home and not to come back. Send an email to the whole company explaining that the Production Team Leader has left the organisation following this week's debacle on the production line. Impaled! Award yourself 10 points.

Terrible leadership is not only effective, it can also be very quick.

b. More interesting is if you can induce Inna to implicate some of her team members. For example, perhaps she says Bob and Glen messed it up because they were meant to be the experts. Now you tell Inna to fire them both when they come back in the morning. Not only do you get a double impaling, you have also made Inna do something she probably feels extremely uncomfortable doing, especially given she has probably acted out of cowardice and self-interest. Double impaling and a psychological battering! Award yourself 20 points.

3. There is a third way, and it is more subtle. Does Inna have something you want? Could she bribe you to keep her job? What could she bribe you with? We are now straying into advanced Terribleness, and you will find out much more on the subject in Chapter 9, but it's always worth considering that today's mess-up might give you a way to something you want in the future...

Another true great from the annals of Terrible Leadership is the Roman Emperor Caligula. Much has been written about Caligula, the horse he promoted to general and his various sexual depravities. Much of it is untrue and part and parcel of the intrigue and shit-slinging of Roman leadership. To be fair to Caligula, much of the really fruity, loopy stuff written about him was written by people who had an agenda against his rule and were writing many years after his death. However, we do know he wasn't one to pass up the opportunity to teach people a lesson and his Terrible reputation is certainly well earned. Caligula wanted his people to see him as a god. Nothing wrong with that at all. Anthony A. Barrett in his authoritative account of the Roman leader[2] recounts:

> *"He is said by Seutonius to have stood beside a statue of Jupiter and to have asked the actor Apelles which of the two was greater. When Apelles hesitated Caligula did indeed have him flayed."*

As a Terrible leader it is important never to let the mistakes of your people go unnoticed. You only get so many opportunities to punish, admonish and generally put your people in their place. Remember, they weren't promoted, you were — so they need to be reminded of this from time to time. Any mistake, no matter how trifling or insignificant, is an opportunity for punishment. Grasp these opportunities, cherish them — they are but fleeting moments of reactive satisfaction in an otherwise proactive reign of tyranny.

> As a Terrible leader it is important never to let the mistakes of your people go unnoticed.

Terrible tip

Keep a list of your favourite punishments and create a roster, ensuring you use each equally and each person on your team gets a good selection of different punishments. There are many ways to teach people a lesson, ranging from physical abuse (throw a stapler at them) to psychological attack (undermine them in front of their peers) — so try and use a varied approach. If you're keen to add flaying to your list of punishments in deference to Caligula, you'd be wise to copy the example of the Hongwu Emperor of China. Zhu Yuanzhang ruled China from 1368 to 1398, and was the founder and first emperor of the Ming Dynasty. The first Ming Emperor brought not only vases to international attention but also the practice of flaying alive (removing the skin of the victim) and slow-slicing (a torturous death by a series of incisions). He once suspected the populace of a town of talking about him in a non-generous way so he ordered 5,000 of the town's womenfolk flayed. Vlad went in for impaling, Zhu liked a spot of flaying. What's your punishment of choice?

Lesson 2: Divide and conquer

In the previous chapter, we looked briefly at the mechanism of 'divide and conquer' as a way of increasing the level of competition in your working environment — thus paving the way for your heightened levels of Terribleness. But who can we turn to from the history books as an exemplar of this approach?

Let's go back to the hero of this whole book — Ivan the Terrible. What he did during his long reign is a master class in how to divide and rule — in fact, his initially inexplicable and very sudden division of Russia into two separate states is one of the master strokes of Terrible leadership of all time. Let's look at what he did, why, what he achieved by doing it and what we can learn from his example.

Ivan was hungry for power and control, as every good Terrible leader should be. He was frustrated by the influence of the land-owning boyars, in much the same way as our hero Vlad the Impaler had been around 100 years before in Wallachia. He felt they did little to support his military efforts, stole from the treasury and oppressed the commoners, creating hardship and unrest. Essentially, he wanted to reduce their power and influence and to do this, he had a cunning plan.

In 1565, he and his family set off on holiday from Moscow. If you are imagining Ivan, Mrs. Terrible and a couple of kids, with perhaps a nanny and some pets, you are widely off the mark. When the Grand Princes of Russia went on 'pilgrimage' they took a huge retinue with them; thousands of people, horses, carts etc. There was something unusual about the way Ivan set out on pilgrimage in 1565, however. His bodyguard was colossal, many times larger than it would normally be, and unusually, he had asked for all of his followers to bring their wives and children. Why would he take so many people with him? You can imagine the unease caused.

> Ivan was hungry for power and control, as every good Terrible leader should be.

People feared the worst, was Ivan coming back? Ivan's fierce, no-nonsense style of leadership was just about all that held Moscow and the whole of Russia together. Without it, law and order would collapse, borders would become fluid and anarchy would reign. People were nervous, and they were right to be.

Ivan went about 100 kilometres to the north-east and from there, sent word that he had decided to resign his post in Moscow and instead he had divided Russia into two parts: the Oprichnina and the Zemshchina. This was most bizarre and something that even today baffles historians. It seemed that Ivan had decided to take a large area including the wealthiest towns surrounding Moscow (but not Moscow itself) and make them into a sort of royal territory where his power would be absolute. This he called the Oprichnina and he appointed its rulers from his most loyal bodyguards. He turned the rest of Russia over to the Boyars, or land owners; this was the Zemshchina.

The Muscovites were terrified. Under the boyars, the ordinary people were likely to be abused and exploited even more, without a state to fall back on and keep the boyars in check. They begged Ivan to come back and he did so, on the condition that his power was absolute in Moscow too, and that he be given total authority to deal with 'trouble makers'. The boyars of Moscow didn't have much choice. Faced with revolt or a returned, more powerful Ivan, they opted for Ivan, and looking back, must have wished they'd gone for revolt, because Ivan's new interpretation of 'trouble maker' was very inclusive. Ivan ruled the Oprichnina with an iron fist. The landowners were gradually banished or disappeared allowing Ivan to give more and more land and wealth to his Oprichniks.

Ivan would eventually re-unite the two parts of his empire but not until the power of the boyars was terminally weakened. He centralised power in Moscow and in him, and dealt harshly with anyone who dared to question his supremacy. By dividing his own realm, he didn't loosen his grip on the Zemshchina (which in reality was a loose network of confederate groups anyway), so much as he tightened his grip on the key strategic area of the Oprichnina. This large area around and to the north-east of Moscow was the bit of Russia that mattered most, and Ivan was quick to spot its strategic significance. He acted not out of a desire to bring peace and harmony to his realm, or to further the economic prosperity of his people, he wasn't motivated by eliminating threats to his leadership. He wanted power in its purest form, the ability to control without question the destiny of others. And to achieve this he needed to divide before he could conquer.

We can take Ivan's lesson and apply it readily in the modern business setting. You'll recognise this scenario: a team of highly-competent people working in a technical area such as finance or IT. The boss is reaching retirement age and suddenly decides to bring their retirement age forward because of ill-health. Not at all uncommon and now we have a leadership vacuum. None of the direct reports of the retiring leader are seen as quite strategic or experienced enough to take on the top job, competent though they are, and you are recruited from outside the organisation to take over. You are now, of course, in a nightmare position. The team loved their old boss because they were a Sissy leader and thought being popular was important (probably explains the ill-health, they probably had too many people vomit all over them). Several of the team thought they had a good chance of getting the top job when the old-timer left so your appointment is seen as unpopular and therefore so are you. Now, obviously, as a Terrible leader, you're not worried about being unpopular and you need to ask yourself, "What would Ivan do?" An Ivan-esque response to this situation might run something along the lines of:

> He wanted power in its purest form, the ability to control without question the destiny of others.

Step 1: Divide the senior people from the junior people. Order a strategic review and demand cost savings of 20%,

with no less than 15% coming from headcount. Ring
fence all the senior positions, insisting that the headcount
reductions come from the bottom half of the organisation.
Find a way of increasing the pay of the most senior people
using some of the cost-savings generated by the headcount
reductions. 'Accidentally' leak a detail or two about
this arrangement and, hey presto, the junior half of the
organisation will hate the senior half.

Step 2: Divide the senior team. Promote three of the
existing senior team to become your only direct reports.
Position them in different locations
and encourage them to create a
strong brand and identity around
the teams you allow them to select.
Make sure they are allocated large
and plush offices so that people can
clearly see that you think they are better than everyone
else. Then 'accidentally' leak information suggesting
it was they who demanded the improvements to
their offices.

> Position is nothing
> without power, so if you
> haven't got it, think
> 'divide and conquer'.

If you take these steps, you will find that the team is no longer
intransigent and difficult to manage. By taking steps like this,
you are getting the team into your harness, and from here, you
can steer and control effectively. Essentially, you are forming a
new power structure, one which you design and can therefore

direct. Remember, position is nothing without power, so if you haven't got it, think 'divide and conquer'.

Lesson 3: Line your pockets

You're not in this leadership position for your health. It's a tough job and that's why they pay you so well to do it. The problem is the pay doesn't reflect the toughness, so part of being a really effective Terrible leader is to make the role pay. And pay properly. Don't listen to all the Sissy rubbish about intrinsic motivation and the desire for meaning in their lives. The only people who are looking for meaning in their lives are the ones who have realised they're never going to get rich. Meaning is a poor substitute for cash. In Chapter 9, we will look at some practical approaches to extracting more than simply your paycheck from your leadership role, but for now let's sit back and marvel at one of the all-time greats. This leader will show us that, in order to be really Terrible, we need to think big. If you're thinking about 'borrowing' stationery supplies from the office, then you need to step outside and sit on the naughty step for a while. That will never amount to much. You need to think much bigger and follow in the footsteps of giants...

In 2004 a German NGO called Transparency International published its list of the 10 most self-enriching leaders of the previous few decades. Of course, the NGO was a Sissy-oriented organisation, most NGOs are, and so it thought it was publishing a list of the most corrupt and least good leaders in recent history. Of course, we know as Terrible leaders that what they actually published was a list of some of the most effective Terrible leaders of recent years. My hero from this list is not the person in the number one position, although President Suharto of Indonesia does warrant special mention here for managing to squirrel away the truly staggering figure of between $15 and $35 billion. You read that right. He managed to siphon off not tens of millions of dollars, but tens of *billions*. You have to get up very early in the morning to find the time to misappropriate that kind of cash. But Suharto was in power for an awfully long time and was broadly popular for much of that. The leader that really catches my Terrible eye from the list is the guy at number two: Philippine President Ferdinand Marcos.

Ferdinand Marcos was born in 1917. He studied law at university and served in the Philippine army during World War Two. He was tangled up at an early age with Terrible deeds, eventually being acquitted of murdering a political rival of his father. This brush with the law gave Filipinos every clue they needed that Ferdinand was not going to be a wallflower. In 1954 he marries Imelda, the one with the thing for shoes, and in 1965 he is elected President. In 21 years in power he manages to siphon off between $5 and $10 billion. Being anti-communist during this period ensures the friendship of the US, who pour plenty of juicy loans into the country. Now, Marcos quite rightly identifies the opportunity. It is only because of his excellent leadership that the US is willing, eager even, to extend these generous loans to the country. It is therefore only right that this, in some small way, should benefit him personally.

Philippine foreign debt stands at around $28 billion, and it is plausible that this amount and more is still sitting in various bank accounts belonging to the Marcos family. Marcos is dead now, although his wife of the 2,700 pairs of shoes is still active in Philippine politics, and he left the Philippines with an interesting legacy. This can be most clearly seen in a 2005 poll where Filipinos were asked to vote for their favourite President. Marcos came out on top.

As well as somewhat inflating his personal pay packet, Marcos was also highly effective. He did more to advance the country's education, health and infrastructure systems than others had previously achieved. He brought, at least initially, stability and peace.

He was popular despite the occasional bit of embezzlement, and easily won a second term. The constitution of the Philippines at the time didn't allow for a third term, but Marcos was onto a good thing and didn't want to take his spoon out of the gravy just yet. So he simply, allegedly, faked an attempted assassination of his defence minister and declared martial law. Under martial law, he suspended the constitution and then re-wrote it saying that he could rule for as long as martial law was required. Eventually, things calmed down and it became clear that martial law was really no longer required, which gave Marcos a new problem. But he was doing really well out of the US loans, so he simply re-wrote the constitution again allowing him to rule for as long as he liked regardless of the insignificant issue of martial law.

Marcos points to a couple of key lessons: firstly, when in power, make the most of it. He found ways of pushing money to his own, his families' and his cronies' bank accounts that are literally staggering. He allowed his family and friends to take over just about every major industry in the country, create monopolies and make huge sums. Under his rule, he managed to concentrate wealth in the Philippines into the hands of the very few.

The second lesson we can learn from Marcos' reign is in prolonging it for as long as you possibly can. Ferdinand and Imelda Marcos only left the Philippines because they absolutely had to. They were chased out and had to escape on a helicopter. When the US asked if they had anything to declare when they reached Hawaii, they found gold bricks in their luggage worth millions. This is how we should all aim to leave our final leadership post, hounded out at the very last minute with the total wealth of the organisation secreted about our person, leaping heroically into a helicopter under a hail of small arms fire (I might be exaggerating here a tiny bit). It took the Philippine government over 18 years to claw back any of the money Marcos had managed to extract, and even then, it was only a fraction. Most of it is long gone.

Marcos teaches us that Terrible leadership is not just about achieving the impossible despite the fecklessness of the people around you. It's also about personal enrichment. We can't all succeed in the way Ferdinand Marcos did, there simply isn't enough money in the world, but just imagine if you could manage 1% of what he did. You'd still be a millionaire many times over. Chapter 9 takes a pragmatic look at what you can do within a modern business context to make the teachings of Ferdinand Marcos work for you. Before reading it I suggest you buy yourself a bigger wallet. Liechtenstein should do the trick...

> This is how we should all aim to leave our final leadership post, hounded out at the very last minute with the total wealth of the organisation secreted about our person.

Lesson 4: Play not to lose

A book about Terrible leadership would not be complete without reference somewhere to Genghis Khan. Born Borjigin Temujin in around 1162, he had a rough life full of fighting, kidnap, struggle and difficulty. What he managed through sheer charisma and force of character was to unite a previously divided Mongol empire. By around 1205 he controlled a sizable area not dissimilar to modern Mongolia today, but Temujin was not satisfied with that. He named himself Genghis Khan and set out to build a truly huge empire stretching from China across Eurasia. The brief lesson I want to draw from his reign however, was not his expansionist tendencies, in fact it is quite the opposite.

Genghis Khan was a looter and a destroyer. In Mongolia, he is remembered as a great hero, so don't for a moment think he was just an uppity thug. He achieved greatness for his country in a way few leaders do. But outside of his Mongolian stronghold, his efforts were not always to grow his territory and his control. His army, like a plague of locusts, would sweep through the lands of his enemies sacking towns and villages, wiping out populations and spoiling arable land. He was even said to have diverted the course of a river in order to wipe out all traces of the main city of one of his enemies. He took what he could carry (often including the women and children as slaves), and sent it back to Mongolia. The rest he destroyed. He was responsible for some of the biggest human massacres in history, with estimates running into the millions of people.

This is a big number today but bear in mind that this was around the beginning of the 13th Century. The total world population then would have only been around 400 million. So, to commit an equivalent level of massacre today, you'd need to kill around 17.5 million. This was something Genghis Khan was quite comfortable achieving annually. Much of the land he ransacked he didn't add to his empire, but he left it so ravaged and depleted that vast swathes of Asia took centuries to recover. Reaching out for a thousand miles from his Mongolian stronghold, Khan created a legend of terror and slaughter that still staggers today in terms of its scale and savagery. He attacked Samarkand in modern-day Uzbekistan, his soldiers using prisoners as body shields. Once it had been taken, the populace was ordered onto the plain where they were killed, pyramids of human heads being raised to celebrate the victory.

At Urgench, also in modern Uzbekistan, one Persian scholar estimated that the Mongols killed over a million people alone.

It is unlikely that Urgench could have mustered a million souls for the Mongols to have killed, but the point is this — Urgench wasn't conquered; it was wiped out. The kingdom it was part of was called Khwarzemia and, by the time Khan was finished, the whole kingdom was reduced to rubble and bones.

> Genghis Khan created a legend of terror and slaughter that still staggers today in terms of its scale and savagery.

The Mongols, and later the Tatars, continued ransacking and raiding from around this time (1207) through to the mid 1400s. During this period, it is estimated that they killed around 45 million people. Only World War Two surpasses what the Mongols managed to notch up in terms of body count. And remember, they did everything by hand. I don't mean to be unnecessarily gruesome but there is a huge difference between killing someone with a gun or a bomb and killing someone with a sword. You really have to want to kill someone to do it with a sword, and it's not quick work either. The Mongols really bent their backs and got stuck in, and they did all of this because of the Terrible leadership of one man. Unsurprising then that just the mention of his name still arouses a kind of morbid fascination 800 years later.

But the lesson we can learn from Genghis Khan is not simply to set your alarm early and start whacking off people's limbs with a suitably sharp implement. It's not a bad lesson at all, but he teaches us something else very interesting. Khan knew that the extent of his control, his empire, was never going to be sufficient to reach the limits of the territories he could ransack. He defeated armies from China to Hungary, areas populated by people who had never heard of each other, far less were they going to be united under the leadership of one man — it was just too big an area to govern effectively for the world of 1210. But did Genghis Khan think, "Well, as I can't rule it, I'll leave it alone"? Of course not, he'd gather his troops, a small army of 30 or 40 thousand or so, and head off to completely wipe out his neighbours. Just because you can't have it why should anyone else? The lesson here is don't *always* play to win, instead play not to lose. Khan couldn't have won the territories he conquered for his own empire but he sure as hell rendered them useless for everyone else.

You can apply this learning to your own development as a Terrible leader. I want you to imagine you are a Commercial Director in a large, international consumer goods company. You look after a given geographical area, let's say S.E. Asia. The next promotion you are looking for is a regional General Manager role, and after that, a position on the board. You are keen that your sales figures are fantastic obviously and many of us would be broadly less interested in the relative sales figures of our colleagues in other regions. But not a Genghis Khan-inspired Terrible leader. Just because you can't control or benefit from the sales figures of your colleagues in these areas, why should they? Remember, if everyone else is doing badly and you are doing well, you will look better. Don't play to win, play not to lose. This subtle shift in mindset begins to usefully refocus your efforts. Instead of working hard to squeeze increasingly marginal improvements in your sales figures think how much more profitable it would be for you to do a bit of raping and pillaging in your colleagues' areas. Genghis Khan was a master of espionage and used spies to comprehensively infiltrate the territory of his neighbours before attacking. You could always do the same. Plant a couple of your people in your colleagues' areas. If you call them 'international assignments' no one will spot them for saboteurs. Keep these people loyal to you with hefty bribes and then, at critical points, have them surreptitiously undermine key deals, or chronically under-order to meet demand peaks. Over a period of months and years, a sustained attack like this will consistently show that only one region performs at or above expected levels — yours.

By playing not to lose rather than to win you use the Genghis Khan approach of pulling down the strength around you rather than attempting to build up your own power to outshine that of others. Muscle is relative. If others are weaker than you then you are, by definition, strong. And we are all attracted to strength. Strength gets results, strength gets promoted. Ultimately the strong do, in the end, win.

> Muscle is relative. If others are weaker than you then you are, by definition, strong.

I could go on. We haven't talked about Attila, Tamerlane, or Mao. Saddam Hussein would have been a great exemplar of Terrible leadership. Some of you might be thinking, "But these examples are all men, is Terrible leadership only for the boys?" How wrong you'd be. Granted, most of the well-known examples of historical Terribleness are male, but there are plenty of less well-known female Terrible leaders, for example. Below I have pulled out a few that collectively teach us a fifth and final Terrible leadership lesson. See if you can spot what it is...

Let's start with Queen Ranavalona of Madagascar. She not only wins the prize for the longest official name of any Terrible leader (she was born Princess Rabodoandrianampoinimerina), she was also a real hero of her time. She ruled from 1828 to her death in 1861, a time of colonialism and various foreign pressures. In particular, she was keen to secure her island's independence from England and France, who both had designs on Madagascar as a way of securing safe passage to India. She ripped up agreements with Britain, the superpower of the time, built up the Madagascan arms industry and saw Christianity for what it was: a political vehicle for gaining spiritual influence on her island. She decreed that any Madagascan caught practicing Christianity would be killed, and had perpetrators strung up on ropes over ravines. If they failed to recant, the ropes would be cut and they would be smashed to pieces on the rocks below.

Or take Queen Mary of England. She wasn't known as Bloody Mary because of her passion for tomato-juice-based cocktails. The only surviving child of the infamous Henry the VIII, she returned England to Catholicism and, in the process, burned at least 300 Protestants at the stake. Then there was Isaebella I of Spain who, together with her husband Ferdinand, created the greatest military superpower of their time (during the late 1400s), but also launched the Spanish Inquisition that tortured hundreds of Jews, Muslims and Protestants, in order to convince them to convert to Catholicism. Any non-Catholics at this time were evicted from the country, a measure which, even in the 1400s, was seen as pretty hard-line.

These three had something in common, and they collaborate here to teach us Lesson 5.

Lesson 5: Make examples

This is a great Terrible leadership lesson that children in Britain learn very early as a result of exposure to a strange story called *Watership Down*. Don't let the fact that the story is about rabbits lull you into a false sense of security. At its heart is a truly terrifying (if you're six years old) character called General Woundwort who shreds the ears of any rabbits that try to escape from his warren, and then parades the bloodied, stump-eared wretch in front of its terrified colleagues. I still dream about General Woundwort. Not right, that rabbit.

> You need to single out a few people and punish them terribly. Everyone else will fall into line beautifully.

But rabbits aside, our three iron ladies, as well as making Margaret Thatcher look like a bit of a wimp, show us the importance of taking drastic action against the few in order to cow the many. This is so important if you are going to become really Terrible. You need to single out a few people and punish them terribly. Everyone else will fall into line beautifully...

Incidentally, looking back at the really Terrible greats of the past, by far the most Terrible person I found was a woman. And, if you want to see just how terrible women leaders can be, just type Elizabeth of Bathory into a search engine, but don't say I didn't warn you, you'll need a strong stomach...

I hope in our little tour we have learnt just a little of what true Terrible leadership really means. Vlad the Impaler shows us how to meet the incompetence of those we are unlucky enough to lead; Ivan the Terrible (there is talk of him becoming a saint!) shows us how to maintain divisions in order to maintain control; Ferdinand Marcos reminds us not to lose sight of the fact that we're not in this for the fun of it, remember to make your leadership role pay properly; Genghis reminds us that it is also about balancing the Marcos urge to acquire things for ourselves with the Terrible instinct to destroy what others have, even if we haven't got a use for it, and; finally, the Terrible ladies remind us to make examples of people as we go. So, as a general rule of thumb, if you find yourself in a difficult situation, at a crossroads or facing a dilemma, I want you to pause, reflect, and think. Summon up the ghosts of Terrible leaders past. You have at your disposal a mighty pantheon of mentors, so ask yourself, *"What would Genghis Khan have done in this situation...?"*

---

[2] *Caligula, the Corruption of Power,* 1989

Chapter Three — Lessons in Terrible

- Every mistake made by a minion is an opportunity to teach someone a lesson. Make people learn from their mistakes.
- Keep a track of your favourite punishments and hand them out on a rota system so that all of your hapless direct reports benefit from each in turn.
- If your control over a team, department or organisation is slipping, get it back by dividing and conquering. Use structure to set people up against each other.
- Line your pockets. Brutalising people isn't just fun, it can be highly lucrative too, watch out for every opportunity and read Chapter 9 for more details.
- Balance lining your pockets with playing not to lose. If you can't fit it in your pockets because you've already stuffed them with blank cheques you've stolen from the finance department, destroy it in order to prevent anyone else from benefitting.
- Make examples of people. And do it properly; mangle their ears, burn them at the stake, damage them unspeakably and irreparably so that others behave themselves in terror-stricken numbness.

In plotting the course to Terrible, we are not alone. Whenever we feel unsure or undecided, we just need to look back in time to summon the lessons of Terrible leaders past.

part two
Terribleness
and you

How are you feeling? Amused at the thought of rampaging across the desolate expanses of the Accounts department laying waste to Reporting and Analysis teams in a Mongol-inspired campaign of terror? Hmmm…It's tempting isn't it, but before you reach for your shotgun, let's take a break from all this Terribleness for just a moment and think.

The Terrible leader in Chapter 1 took back the term Terrible. Reading it over again, I do get a twitch, a sensation, a slight longing when it comes to that feeling of power. You need to be careful with leadership. With the role comes responsibility and accountability for the performance of others. I see far too many leaders, especially junior leaders in their first leadership role, get too interested in the power aspect of leadership. Be cautious if that sensation of power appeals too strongly. Remember, the really clever people are the people who make, sell, service, innovate, maintain (etc.) the product, whatever that might be — they make the money/provide the service. They do it, not you. You are there to help them do it to the very best of their ability. And often, their ability is greater than they believe it to be, your task being to unlock that extra capacity and capability. The term 'servant leadership' nicely describes the tone great leaders take when it comes to power. Yes, they are decisive and take control when things get tough or we hit a crisis, but otherwise, they see themselves there to support others.

In Chapter 2, the Terrible leader manages to skew one of the most important leadership lessons out there. As leaders we are here to manage through uncertainty, to help people find an anchor in stormy seas, to remind them of what is fixed when everything seems to have come loose. The last thing you should do as a leader is to accentuate uncertainty! People can handle change phenomenally well. What they normally struggle with is the uncertainty around transition. Are we? Aren't we? It's the false starts, the false dawns and the false certainties that are the stuff of despond. As leaders we are here to do, essentially, two things: manage current levels of performance, and manage change. Initially, you will have enough on your plate to manage the first aspect of leadership, keeping up or improving current levels of performance. With time and competence comes the second part. This is the time when you will need to create a sense of certainty around the change you are leading, a coherent story about what is changing and why, and encourage your people relentlessly as they take their first faltering steps into your new reality.

The Terrible leader also spends a lot of time creating far too much internal competition. It is important to encourage a competitive spirit in many organisations and industries (not all — it can drive rather short-sighted behaviour) BUT make sure the earnest competition is with other organisations where it should be! Sure, have a washing-up competition with the guys in IT, but keep the real energy for your actual competitors.

In Chapter 3, it should be pretty obvious that I am not actually supporting the leadership techniques of Stalin and Vlad the Impaler. But where the Terrible leader misses the point, we can learn. Vlad impaled people. We can do the opposite. When our people make mistakes, we can learn to encourage them and support them. There are two types of mistakes:

1. Stupid ones as a result of not concentrating. Like, if I drop a marmoset into the middle of this paragraph. There it is. Marmoset. That's just sloppy. I have admonished myself in a suitably strong tone and I promise it won't happen again.

2. Mistakes through trying something new or difficult. Think how you'd feel if you got 'told off' in this situation. Pretty awful, but as a leader, you can change someone's life if they've just failed as a result of pushing themselves to do something new. You can congratulate them. They'll get back up and try harder the next time. Get them to think

about what happened and why it went wrong, dust them down, pat them on the back and let them have another crack. Of course, this doesn't work if the task in question is open heart surgery...

Ivan the Terrible caused all kinds of confusion by dividing and conquering his realm. By setting groups up against each other, he assured his own dominance. Again, this is a lesson we can quite easily reverse by considering what we can do to strengthen the unity of our team(s). Silos are almost never good (I appreciate boundaries need to exist in some areas to ensure levels of independence, but those situations aside...). Look at your team today. Do they work as closely as they could? What can you do to bring them together? Two forces keep teams and individuals apart:

1. A sense of competition, or "Me and my team are better than you and your team, so neener neener neener". This sensation is born on the playground and lingers long into the boardroom. It's childish and silly, but boy oh boy, it persists. Try and focus people on what unites them (organisational/ departmental goals). Talk up the positive impact of other teams and people. Help your people to see things from other people's perspectives. Open their eyes...

2. A sense of defensiveness, or "That's my job so get your hands off". This is also known as, "Mine!" I

wonder how many children's first word is 'mine'?
It certainly seems to be the knee-jerk reaction
of many people in the business world. It doesn't
help. Again, encourage your team to welcome
in outsiders, to 'share and play nicely'. It is only
when we learn from others that we run the risk of
getting better at what we do...

I've tried reversing the lesson of Ferdinand Marcos a couple of times. It's an interesting one and it points back to that sense of servant leadership from Chapter 1. Marcos must have had many positive, worthwhile intentions. He was, after all, very popular and achieved much for the Philippines. Somewhere along the line, though, he got personally greedy. If this becomes a temptation for you, STOP. Just don't do this. Leadership should be about what you can give to others, not about what you can get for yourself. If you don't see that, the irony is, you'll not get very far with leadership, so the system has an in-built balance. Marcos was on the make, and I meet loads of leaders who seem fascinated by how to 'get ahead'. For them, progress through and up an organisation is the game they are playing, and they see it as a web of relationships they need to develop, senior stakeholders they need to influence etc. I can't help but get a bit depressed with this approach. Instead, I would always recommend focusing on what you believe you and your team can achieve for the organisation. Make this big and brave and then figure out how to make it happen, while at the same time making as many people look fabulously successful along the way. The promotions will look after themselves...

Then there's good old Genghis. A straightforward one to reverse, this. Rather than ruin or destroy the things others could put to good use (but that you can't use personally), try building them up instead. Look out for opportunities for others to get ahead. Send colleagues the best members of your team to help them out when you know they're in a pinch, without having to be asked. 'Your area' isn't 'your area' at all. It is just the area, owned by your business, that you have been asked to temporarily steward. So treat it that way.

The ladies that made examples of others got it right, but focused on the negative instead of the positive. It is absolutely the right thing to do to make examples of people, so when someone does something that really impresses you, whether absolutely (they hit a big number) or relatively (they hit a small number having hit nothing for months because they were learning), throw them a party. I mean it. A party. Invite the whole team to your house, bake a cake, open a bottle of champagne (or 27) and enjoy each other's company, while remembering to say some nice things about the person who impressed you and why. People will be falling over to work with you.

Ok, I hope that has reset your sense of decency and propriety. You are about to delve back into a dark and Terrible world. And this time it's personal...

CHAPTER 4
HOW TERRIBLE ARE YOU?

So far, in this book, we have looked at explaining Terribleness and we have reclaimed the term 'Terrible' as a model for our own leadership. We have checked to see that, as an approach, it is appropriate and timely within our modern 21st Century context. And it is. We have turned back the years and revelled in the true genius of some of the greats of Terribleness. We have seen that there is much to learn when it comes to attaining true Terribleness and that most of us are puny indeed when compared to the heights attained by many of history's exemplars.

But how Terrible are you today? There are five possible conditions you are likely to find yourself in:

1. You were born on the road to tyranny. You're already so tyrannical that you probably don't even see this road as a road. A road suggests a conscious choice, like a path. You were not aware of making a choice, you just turn up to work and start ripping people to shreds. That's just normal behaviour, isn't it?

2. You are well down the road to tyranny. You may have been a fully-fledged Sissy, or a dabbler in the dark art of Terrible leadership, but now you are

on course and reaping the rewards of your most excellent decision.

3. You are at the start of the road to tyranny. It looks a little daunting, like a members-only club where lots of people seem to be wearing cardigans. You're not sure if this is for you...

4. Your satnav just doesn't seem to pick up the road to tyranny. You'd like to find it, but every time you look for the road, you seem to end up in the wrong lane, heading back towards polite chit-chat and showing concern about the health of people's pets.

5. You can see the road and you have made the (strange) decision it is not for you. You are turning your back on Terribleness. This is fine by us, that gives us a perfect view of where to stick the knife.

One of those probably describes where you find yourself today and you may well wish to pursue the path to full Terribleness further. But how to tell if you are becoming increasingly Terrible or just staying the same? Stephen Covey in his seminal work *The Seven Habits of Successful People* stated that a key habit was continual personal development (or 'sharpening the saw' as he put it). While obviously Covey's book is mostly full of Sissy advice, I do agree with the need to constantly monitor your level of Terribleness and look to improve upon it day by day. The old adage is true: what you can't measure you can't manage. If only there were some sort of Terribleness gauge, some way of discerning your true Terribleness quotient...

> You need to constantly monitor your level of Terribleness and look to improve upon it day by day.

When setting out to write a book on leadership, Terrible or otherwise, there is something they don't tell you. It's like some sort of Magic Circle thing — listen carefully and I will let you in on a little secret. Late one night, it was probably misty and there might have been an owl hooting, I could swear I sensed someone following me home. Living in central London, this is not altogether an uncommon experience, but you do typically get a little more flustered when they follow you up your garden path. After bundling me through my front door, the stranger pulled back their cloak to reveal a balding, sweaty man with crooked teeth. It was an average Englishman! Less average was the knife he was brandishing close to my throat. And all he said before he turned on his heel back into the mist was, "Make sure it's got a questionnaire in it". "In what?" I asked, quite reasonably I thought. "The book, you idiot," came the reply over his shoulder and he was gone.

You see, if you don't have a questionnaire in a book like this, bad things happen to you, as the informative pamphlet he left behind described. Total lack of any questionnaire and he would come back with some 'heavies' and break my legs. A badly researched questionnaire and he'd send a dog round to bite my ankles each morning on the way to the station for a week. Irritating... so...

On the next few pages you will find the TQ test. It's much like an IQ test, but for Terribleness. Take it to discern your TQ today. Unlike IQ, TQ can change over time (remember, Darth Vader didn't start out totally Terrible, but he improved with age) so, ideally, you would self-administer this test every six to 12 months to determine whether or not your TQ was flourishing.

Perhaps you could keep a track of your scores on some sort of graph and pin it up prominently in your office. Set yourself a target and use the tips in Chapter 5 to help you improve your scores. But — before we get to thinking about improving Terribleness, let's get an early marker on your innate, background level of Terribleness. Don't worry too much if your TQ isn't very high at the moment — it's early days and you haven't finished this book yet.

Now remember, the TQ test is *highly* scientific and has been developed over a long period, including coffee, a Danish pastry and several cold beers. You should take the results highly seriously and remember that they are highly accurate and scientific. If you don't believe me, I can use words like 'domain' and 'manifold', if that helps. See how you get on...

'Doctor' Dan's 'patented' Terribleness Quotient Questionnaire

Instructions: Answer the questions in the way that is most representative of you and reflects what you would actually do. Some people say they behave differently at home and at work and wonder with which 'hat' on they should answer these kinds of questionnaires. To get a good measure of Terribleness, I would suggest the best hat would be something with a point on the top — as these are nearly always worn by the bad guys (e.g. the Klan, the Nazis, Priests etc.).

Question 1: In an average year, what is the value (in US$) of the office furniture you break as a result of spectacular shows of anger (e.g. throwing chairs, pounding desks etc.)?

    A: $10,000+   B: $5,000 – $10,000

    C: $1,000 – $5,000   D: $100 – $1,000

    E: Less than $100

Question 2: When you throw something (let's say, for example, a stapler) at an employee to demonstrate your dissatisfaction with their performance, do you aim for:

    A: Eyes   B: Head.   C: Body   D: Aim to miss

    E: I don't throw things at employees, at least not
       hard things.

Question 3: What would be your ideal pet?

    A: A leopard or a whale

    B: Pitbull terrier or a Rottweiler

    C: An ill-tempered Daschund

    D: A duck

    E: A kitten

Question 4: You see an old lady struggling with her bags up some stairs. Do you:

    A: Take the opportunity to mug her and run off with her purse.

    B: Shout at some feckless youth to help the old bag and admonish them for not having done it faster, remembering to upbraid the old witch for being a drain on resources.

    C: Help her after negotiating a significant fee for your help.

    D: Ignore her.

    E: Help her.

Question 5: What's your favourite colour?

    A: Death and destruction black

    B: Illness and major nuisance brown

    C: Gloomy grey

    D: Daft blue

    E: All the colours of the rainbow are my favourite!

Question 6: On holiday I like to:

    A: Relax and unwind by taking part in illegal coups in Africa OR smuggling conflict diamonds.

    B: Relax and unwind by stalking enemies.

    C: Relax and unwind by shooting lots of small fluffy animals.

    D: Relax and unwind by being rude to the hotel staff.

    E: Relax and unwind by taking bracing walks by the sea.

Question 7: Someone cuts very close in front of you while driving, causing you to brake suddenly and giving you a fright. Do you:

    A: Follow them to their house and murder them and their entire family.

    B: Follow them very closely until they are going round a corner and drive into the back of them thus pushing them off the road and destroying their car, possibly causing serious injury as well.

    C: Overtake them and then cut back in front of them even closer.

    D: Honk maniacally on your horn, flash your lights and drive very aggressively behind them for a few minutes.

    E: Back off, shrug and think, "This guy is tired of living!"

Question 8: Your spouse (or cleaner) has accidentally washed your favourite jeans in the wrong wash and they are now a faded pink colour. Do you:

   A: Feed the guilty party into a giant-sized industrial washing machine with lots of red dye to illustrate the point that although "it's only a slight change in colour", this does make a big difference.

   B: Wait for them to go out and then put all their favourite white tops in a wash with a beetroot.

   C: Make a point of wearing the disgusting jeans to social events where they want you to look good.

   D: Shout at them for being a useless and careless person, suggesting a link to an underlying character deficit in some way.

   E: Hey ho! Accidents happen – you just roll your eyes and say, "Well it's an excuse to go shopping!"

Question 9: A member of your team comes to you with a request for training. Do you:

   A: Sack them. They are clearly incompetent and unable to do the job, otherwise they wouldn't need training.

   B: Offer them the choice of training or bonus. If they opt for the bonus, don't give it to them as they are clearly not skilled enough to warrant one.

   C: Point out that you didn't need any training to get to where you are and that they should spend more

time worrying about their rather underwhelming
performance than dreaming up training schemes
to attend.

D: Sigh loudly and remind them about the pressure
the internal departmental training budget is
under. Tell them you'll think about it. Don't.

E: Respond enthusiastically and ask them to attend
and bring back their insights for the rest of
the team.

Question 10: It's the end of the world as we know it. There has
been some sort of catastrophe, possibly human-induced, possibly
not, perhaps a rogue asteroid. There are not many people left
and those that remain are mostly disfigured or messed up in
some way. Thankfully you're alright, and best of all, your iPod
still works! Do you:

A: Find a load of guns and set up your own kingdom
where subjects must comply with your every
deviant whim. You kill anyone who steps out of
line and sleep with all the best-looking ones who
aren't too messed up.

B: You go a bit mental and drive around like a
character out of *Mad Max*, stealing and killing
indiscriminately.

C: You keep to yourself and spend your time playing
golf and drinking all the good wine you can find.
You only interact with others to steal their food.

D: You join up with a band of survivors and seem nice enough but secretly plot to take over and sleep with all the best-looking ones who aren't too messed up.

E: You join up with a band of survivors and work tirelessly to take care of the more messed up ones and strive to create a 'new beginning' on this shattered planet. You are probably quite stoic and reliable.

Interpreting your results:

Award yourself points on the following scale:

A = 5 Terrible points

B = 4 Terrible points

C = 3 Terrible points

D = 2 Terrible points

E = 1 Terrible point

If you scored...

40–50 Terrible points: Ivan the Terrible will be round shortly, not to congratulate you, but to decapitate you. You are a serious threat to his position as the most Terrible leader in history.

30–40 Terrible points: Well done — this is sterling work, you are clearly Terrible to the core and have a bright and Terrible future ahead of you. Consider how you could add polish and occasional élan to your already impressive Terribleness.

20–30 Terrible points: Don't give up hope! You clearly have some inner Sissy to cripple (remember — back of the knees) but there is a Terrible leader in you just trying to get out. Read on to discover how to nurture it...

10–20 Terrible points: Oh dear. Very disappointing. Hang your head in shame. Simply must try harder etc. etc. Perhaps buying more Terrible leader books would help. It'll be a long climb from here but, as any Terrible leader knows, there is nothing that can't be learnt. Unless you're a muppet. In that case, you're doomed.

Less than 10 Terrible points: Your maths is less than impressive.

So — there you go, you have your Terribleness 'low water' mark. It can only get better from here on. As you practice the art of Terribleness, you will find that your attitude and views change subtly. Whereas today you answered E or D, you will find in the future that to do so will be ridiculous and that C or B is obviously the right answer. In most questionnaires, there is no right or wrong answer, it is just a question of different styles — we all have different gifts etc. What a load of rubbish — clearly A was the right answer in all of the above. If you look back now I think you'll agree it will seem obvious. But as with so many things, it is only obvious in hindsight. Don't worry, if you scored low (anything under about 25), help is at hand. The next chapter is dedicated to the daily routines and rituals you can instil to help yourself become more Terrible day by day...

Chapter Four — Lessons in Terrible

- Measure your innate Terribleness now, and then again every six months or so to track progress.
- Buy a pointy hat.
- Throw more office furniture at people.
- Buy a leopard.
- Sack your cat.

For handy hints and tips on how to keep a leopard, try: *www.ohmygodmycatkeptgrowing.com.*

CHAPTER 5
TOWARDS TERRIBLE DAY BY DAY

Obviously, each chapter of this book is equally important — but not this one. This one is most important. Here, we will look at the routines and disciplines you need to become truly Terrible. We will look at the simple exercises you can build into your daily life that will enhance your innate Terribleness and build new Terribleness muscles. Follow this practical advice and you'll be instilling fear and terror in surprisingly little time. To do this, we need to look at the little things that the truly Terrible do. As they say, the devil is in the detail and this has never been so true. To tyrannise effectively, you need to pay attention to the small things...

To do this, we will enter the daily life of an advanced Terrible leader. They are purely fictional. Let's call them Gordon. Let's imagine Gordon has a high-profile job in a government department, perhaps with several thousand minions reporting to him, and a budget of several hundred million pounds. Or dollars! There's no reason of course why this imaginary Gordon might not be spending dollars or Euros or anything else.

Gordon works very hard and balances his tough day job with the demands of family life (he has a wife and two children). He is successful, respected and has even been linked with his boss's job, although frustratingly for Gordon, his boss seems pretty intent on hanging around. But don't be fooled, Gordon is no Sissy leader. Gordon is Terrible to the core. When people hear Gordon is on the way, they check to see if they have sturdy undergarments on. And if they don't, they rush out and buy some. So, using this *entirely fictitious* case study, what can we learn about the daily life of a Terrible leader? (I cannot, nor can my lawyers, state strongly enough that this case study is pure fabrication and any resemblance to real people or events is entirely coincidental.)

> When people hear Gordon is on the way, they check to see if they have sturdy undergarments on.

The alarm bell rings. It is 5am. Terrible leaders rise early. There are birds singing outside and the sideways light of a summer morning is filtering through the curtains which suck back and forth with barely a rustle in a light breeze. Gordon hits the alarm to off and lies back as his wife nuzzles in, suggesting five more minutes would be a good idea. Gordon, in many ways, would like nothing more than to throw an arm around her and dive back under the duvet for another hour or more, but this is not the way of the Terrible. Gordon manfully throws back the duvet and swings his legs off the bed, crashing his left knee into his bedside table and knocking a glass of water all over some important papers. One foot impales itself on a particularly spiky Lego brick. Gordon smiles ruefully — it's going to be a Terrible day. Conscious for only 30 seconds, he has already captured the mood he is looking for.

You see, most of us simply get up in the morning. Not the truly Terrible. They manage and engineer every aspect of their days to ensure maximum Terribleness can be achieved with the minimum of effort. Gordon used to consciously leave obstacles in the path of his early morning rituals, but by now, it has become second nature. A well placed piece of furniture, a plate of bread and jam on the floor, even some of your children's toys — they can all serve as worthy adversaries before your brain has begun to fully function. Gordon knows to not fully trust himself to be on his 'A-game' from the get go, but with his care and attention to detail, he is ready to attend to his first point of business for the day.

> The truly Terrible manage and engineer every aspect of their days to ensure maximum Terribleness can be achieved.

Gordon makes his way downstairs to the office. It is small, but he only uses it first thing in the morning and at weekends. He fires up his computer and consults the same spreadsheet he consults every morning. On it, he keeps a careful, colour-coded record of his early morning calls. Across the top are a series of time slots ranging from 3am to 6am. The 3am slot is an angry red, receding to a mild mustard colour for 6am. On today's date, he is scheduled for a 5am call to Mike, his press secretary. Mike doesn't know this and is very likely still asleep. Gordon consults another column to see what Mike has received by way of early morning calls in recent months. He's had a 3am 'missing email' call and a 6am 'go to a city a long way away' call. The schedule indicates Mike has not received a 'random rant' or an 'obscure/unachievable request' call for quite some time. Gordon selects 'random rant' and scrolls through a list of potential topics before dialling Mike's number from his desk phone. "Mike, did I wake you? Good. It's time we talked about the quality of your work...."

This is advanced Terribleness. Gordon doesn't leave his early morning calls to chance. Instead, there is a detailed schedule of who has received what and when. This way, Gordon can be sure people are treated equally, thus avoiding favouritism. Every member of his leadership team will periodically get a call or a left message at a similarly unsociable time with topics ranging from their personal competence to impossible tasks. Gordon really cares about his own Terribleness, he manages it with real attention. He understands that these calls create real 'edge' within the team, thus obviously driving a high performing environment where everyone strives to do their very best. But what does our Terrible leader do next...?

> Gordon really cares about his own Terribleness, he manages it with real attention.

Gordon slams the phone down while Mike is still making some feeble argument and wanders downstairs to make coffee and eat toast. The morning's papers have yet to be delivered — they are due at 5.30am. It is 5.35am. Gordon doesn't miss a beat. Armed with a piece of toast, slippers and his pyjamas, he leaves the house and goes three doors down the road to the newsagent. Spewing toast crumbs like an Icelandic volcano, he berates the owner of the newsagent for an appalling lack of service. He picks up the copies of the papers that are overdue at his house and threatens to cancel his subscription before stalking back up the road to his still open front door. The paper boy is coming round the corner. Catching Gordon's eye, he begins backpedalling, but not before Gordon has had a chance to roll up one of the more left-wing newspapers and hurl it at him along with some general remarks regarding the moral character of people who are habitually late.

It is 5.45am and Gordon has already inflicted three cases of Terribleness. Can you keep up, because he doesn't let up. What's important to notice here is the flexible aspect of true Terribleness. Yes, you can schedule aspects of your day to accentuate your innate Terribleness, but watch too for the unexpected, unplanned for opportunities. Make life difficult for yourself in order to generate the required ire to inflict tyranny, but never miss an opportunity to make life difficult for others. The newsagent will now have a whole load of angst and anguish ready and primed to unleash at the hapless (and probably useless) paper boy when he returns from his round. In many ways Gordon has done him a favour. A few more instances like this and the newsagent will probably sack the paper boy, get a better one and have happier, more loyal customers as a result. You see, Terribleness is about *getting results* — fast. Let's see what Gordon is up to now...

It's 8.40am. Gordon has made his way to the office. The taxi was late so whilst being driven in, Gordon phoned and complained about him loudly to the taxi company, remembering not just to complain about the tardiness but also the strange

smell in the car. He was given a discount on
his next week's fares. Now, his secretary has
arrived to talk him through his day. His first
meeting is at 9am with a peer from another
department. Sue has been trying to get in his
diary for a long time to discuss collaboration

> Never miss an opportunity to make life difficult for others.

between their respective departments. Gordon judiciously asks
his secretary to move the meeting to 4pm when he was due to
'walk the floor'. Gordon knows full well that his secretary will
have warned his management team about this so by postponing
Sue he not only makes her feel insignificant and frustrated,
he also engineers the opportunity to spring his 'walking the
floor' exercise early. From 9–10am he wanders around the
building leaning on people's desks and asking them challenging
questions, "What's your position on x?" or "How many of these
have you done this month?". Everyone stutters and stumbles
through incoherent answers as best as they can. Gordon stares at
each person at the end of this performance and shakes his head
slowly before moving on. If he's feeling playful, he might add
some tutting. If someone strings together something vaguely
sensible, Gordon takes out a pen and makes a note in his book
and frowns menacingly. He enjoys this process — the results
are immediate and it is very gratifying cutting across layers of
hierarchy like this. He even pops into the post room and looks
disapprovingly for a moment at the mess on the desk.

There are two important lessons for aspiring Terrible leaders
here in terms of your everyday activity. Gordon has 'gone to the

source' as they say in Sissy management handbooks. While it is very important to tyrannise your direct reports, Gordon knows that to create the ultimate high-performance environment, it is important that his shadow is cast right down the organisation. There is no better way of doing this than by getting out there and intimidating the staff. They are not hard to intimidate as they are normally bad at their jobs and are trying to cover it up. Gordon knows this and tolerates it, as confident employees would just be more likely to stir up unrest and other problems.

> They are not hard to intimidate as they are normally bad at their jobs and are trying to cover it up.

Try and get out for 10 minutes every day, or an hour once a week. You will be amazed at the results it can bring. Make sure to arrive unexpectedly and suddenly at people's desks. Loom over them and don't suggest they stand up, ideally they will stay in their seats as you tower above them. Keep the high ground. Even if you do know their name, make a point of starting with, "Soooo (very obviously check name plate on desk) Steve...". Then ask them difficult questions they are unlikely to have thought about in any detail, the more obscure and theoretical the better. Select from:

1.   What, in your view, are the three most important functions of this department?

2.   In your opinion, within the Generation Y context, how can we most effectively rationalise the cost of the customer experience?

3.   Do you think we should allow pets in the office?

4.   What have you done in your personal life to support the Kyoto protocol?
5.   How does the recent change in departmental structures affect staffing priorities for the next 12 months?

If you are really having fun you could always try:
6.   What do you feel I could do better as your leader?

This last one will really make them squirm. You can use positive body language to suggest, erroneously, that you want them to give an honest response. Nods, a smile, some expectant puppy dog eyes should do it. Obviously, then have their manager fire them if they say anything challenging or disrespectful. This will soon get round the office, so you'll probably only be able to pull the trigger on this one a couple of times, but from then on, you will always get lots of effusive praise when asking this question. Which is nice. Once people have given their pathetic answers to your questions, your best policy is not to ask further questions, this gives them time to think and clarify. Best instead to turn on your heel, stalk off and find the next victim, or 'employee' if you are still 'thinking Sissy'.

The second lesson to learn here is the importance of good diary management. Most of you will put things in your diary and then do those things. Gordon knows that this is a puny way to conceptualise one's diary, and that there is a lot to be gained from creative diary management. Sue was expecting to see him at 9am. By moving the meeting at the very last minute

(Sue might have already been on her way), Gordon is not-so-subtly letting Sue know that he is more important and more ruthless than she is. When it comes to the actual discussion about inter-departmental collaboration, Gordon now knows he will have the upper hand, and will almost certainly win the eventual negotiations. The Terrible leader is always aware of the unwritten, alert to the unsaid. Discussions concerning inter-departmental collaboration is short-hand for 'getting your department to do the crappy work we don't want to do'. Truly Terrible leaders know this and respond appropriately, as we shall see later...

> The Terrible leader is always aware of the unwritten, alert to the unsaid.

It's 10.18am and Gordon is 18 minutes late for the quarterly finance review. His chief finance officer is nervous. He is supposed to have found 15% of cost savings for the year to date and is several percentage points adrift. He explains the reasons for this, the caveats around the numbers and the actions they are taking to remedy the situation as best he can. Gordon responds positively, this is understandable, he knows they've all done their best etc. The meeting goes far better than the CFO expects. Initially, he is suspicious, this is very unlike Gordon and experience tells him not to get too excited just yet. But at 10.59, a mild elation starts to settle in and he relaxes and even stops sweating and starts to smile a little. It is now when Gordon springs his trap. "Keep up the good work, and whatever we're short of at the end of the year we'll recoup through headcount reductions in the Finance department —

enjoy the rest of your day. Goodbye." The CFO wonders if this is a joke and tests this out with a nervous laugh. Gordon quite rightly responds thunderously, slamming his fist onto the desk and knocking over a nearby chair, "You think this is a joke, something to laugh about? How dare you, your incompetence etc etc." The CFO and his retinue of accountants and analysts walk briskly away, trembling and pale. You can guarantee there are going to be plenty of pizzas being delivered to the finance department later this evening...

Here, Gordon shows us the importance of managing expectations. As a fully-fledged Terrible leader, people expect Gordon to be Terrible. This can somewhat dull the experience of Terribleness for your employees. The truly Terrible appreciate this conundrum, i.e. they have become almost too good at their jobs. Just because you have become too good at what you do doesn't mean others should suffer, so Gordon very considerately here demonstrates the ability to create behavioural contrasts. Initially he is warm and understanding, lulling the CFO and his cronies into a false sense of security. Gordon is like a python, slowly coiling around his prey. Initially, the prey item, or CFO in this instance, is wary, ready to jump away. But Gordon relaxes his coils, and accordingly so does the prey. Before he knows it, the CFO is almost enjoying Gordon's scaly embrace. It is at precisely this point, when the prey item has forgotten the true power of the coils surrounding it, that the Terrible leader knows to apply the pressure, hard. The impact of this can be so startling, so alarming, so severe that it can drive the most

> It is at precisely this point, when the prey item has forgotten the true power of the coils surrounding it, that the Terrible leader knows to apply the pressure, hard.

fantastical behavioural responses. It is quite plausible that the CFO won't go home for three days in a stress-induced orgy of overtime now. If they don't have a breakdown then they are made of the right stuff; if they crash and burn they can normally be disposed of (talk to HR) and they were clearly unfit for the job anyway. This advanced Terrible behaviour is known as 'talent management'. This is not straightforward, it takes real effort to go from sweetness and light to thunder and lightning in a couple of seconds, but the greats appreciate this is the only way to separate the wheat from the chaff, the haves from the have-nots, the winners from the losers. This is a fine point to grasp and understand, but let's return for a moment to the wider lesson. To accentuate your Terribleness, it helps if you can contrast it with some 'fake Sissy' behaviour. This way, your people will fully appreciate the range and depth of your Terribleness and they won't take you for granted.

At 11am, Gordon's car is ready to take him over to another building for a joint meeting of departmental heads for a briefing from a series of security advisors on some emerging threat or other. He uses the time in the car to make a series of three brief phone calls, two to turn the heat up on a couple of strategic projects, demanding updates for that afternoon, and the third to his wife to remind her to pick up his dry cleaning. At 11.34, Gordon arrives at the meeting, which is due to start at 11.45.

Everyone else is there already and Gordon takes the opportunity to indulge in some slightly indiscreet banter about who he'd seen at a golf club over the weekend. At 11.45, the advisors are ushered in and the briefing begins. After twenty minutes or so, the advisors are drawing their briefing to a close. A few people ask interested and sensible questions. Gordon bides his time. The questions are answered and after about forty minutes, the meeting is beginning to look like it will wrap up on time at 12.30. It is at this point that Gordon strikes.

He asks a couple of questions about the validity of the source information. These are satisfactorily answered, although clearly the analysts are unimpressed with the insinuation. Gordon then pulls out of his bag a report procured by one of his aides that concludes contradictory findings to the advisors in front of him and asks them to explain this. The advisors are clearly stumped, one of them has been broadsided and knows nothing about this other report. The other one attempts to explain, badly, the rationale behind the two findings. His stuttering answer brings on other questions from the assembled audience. Gordon lets others fire in clarifying questions for 10 minutes or so, enjoying the smell of blood in his nostrils. At about 12.35, he cuts across one of the special advisors and states that, immensely enjoyable though it is to listen to the ill-informed, he really is not interested in wasting his time any further and that he has far more important things to be taking care of in his department. Immediately, he stands up and walks out of the room. You can guarantee nothing of much interest or importance will be said after he has left and that the session will wrap up shortly afterwards.

This is a masterpiece of Terribleness, quite perfect in every way and you too can utilise some of this behaviour in your everyday life. Firstly, remember this: it is much easier to pull down than to build up. Cherish your inner critic. Use it to pour scorn, doubt, ridicule and delay on the not-so-bright idea of others. If you play cards you will know that it is much easier to play to lose than to play to win, and the same is true in leadership. Much better to undermine the position of others, and thus assume a dominant position, rather than to try and build a dominant position all on your own.

> Much better to undermine the position of others, and thus assume a dominant position, rather than to try and build a dominant position all on your own.

Essentially, there are two ways to influence other people: make your idea look good (difficult and time consuming) or make their idea look bad (quick and easy). Really, it's a no-brainer. In this instance, Gordon illustrates the point beautifully. He also points to another critical component in undermining the ideas of others: do it late in the meeting. Before torpedoing other people's advice or ideas, it is best to hear them out — don't show your hand too early, or they will have time to work out a counter-argument. The other Terrible lesson we can learn for everyday use from this little vignette could perhaps best be summarised as, 'the meeting isn't happening if I'm not in the room'. Turn up late, leave early, do whatever it takes to make the point that you are the most important person in the room and that if you're not there then there really isn't much point in carrying on. This is something so simple you can actively start working on it tomorrow — just think of all the time you could claw back if you left every meeting 10 minutes early or arrived 10 minutes late, or *both*!

By 1pm, Gordon is back at his office in time for a lunch appointment with his boss. They work in the same building and have arranged to meet at reception, and although Gordon arrives back at 12.55, he waits around the corner in the car until 1pm sharp before appearing. He ushers his boss outside to the waiting car and has arranged a good table at the best restaurant in the area which he knows his boss is particularly fond of. A good bottle of wine, glowing reports of progress and rapturous laughter at all of his boss's lame jokes ensures that the lunchtime session is a great success. In fact, his boss is so impressed by Gordon's unflinching command of his area and the great results he is clearly delivering that he asks him to think about taking on additional responsibility, perhaps another department or two. Gordon appears serious, and talks about the important phase his department is going through, the need to stay the course and a desire to see things through. And, at the same time, strongly intimates he'd be more than willing to consider it, for the right remuneration package obviously. His boss asks Gordon about potential successors to him at his current department if he were to take a step up. In Gordon's mind's eye, he sees the CFO being lowered into a hole. Gordon answers by saying that though his leadership team is still largely dependent on him for most of the difficult or important decisions, he suspects someone could be got ready. He is careful not to mention any names but ensures his boss that he could have something worked out in a couple of months. They part on excellent terms and long handshakes. Their cars arrive, Gordon's to take him back to his office, and the boss's car to take him off to a golf appointment with some important diplomats. All is well in the world and Gordon gives his bag to his driver and decides to walk the fifteen minutes or so back to the office along the river.

There is a fundamental truth here about Terribleness. It may not be immediately applicable, but it is worth preparing yourself for. The more Terrible you become, the more opportunity will be placed in front of you. The longer, greater and more chilling the shadow you cast, the more senior people will want to have you working for them. They can smell the power you exude, you will be giving it off like a pheromone and like moths to a candle, they will flutter in to feed on your energy, vigour and results. Let them come. Try to show a willingness to proceed with the caution appropriate of the true professional. Let it be obvious you are keen for more responsibility, provided a proper job can be done. Try and link your own compensation considerations to this desire to do a proper job. e.g. never 'act' up a level, it shows weakness and a willingness to do work you're not paid to do. Try intimating that to do the job properly, you'll need the authority, and therefore the position, and therefore the pay.

The other lesson here is very simple and one you'll almost certainly know anyway — *make your boss like you*. The Terrible leader knows that they must do whatever it takes to ensure the boss

> The more Terrible you become, the more opportunity will be placed in front of you.

thinks favourably of them. Sure, you might stab them in the back once you have the sufficient authority, but on the way up, exercise every deferential, sycophantic muscle you can. They will say they don't want to be surrounded by sycophants. The best way to interpret this is as follows, "*I **do** want to be surrounded by sycophants*". This is reverse psychology from the Brere Rabbit school, "Please suh, don't throw me in that there briar patch". Don't believe a word of it. You will soon get a sense of how best to manipulate the boss.

Gifts can work well, but be careful not to stray into anything that looks like outright bribes unless your boss clearly intimates that they would respond well to this sort of behaviour. In more enlightened countries (Russia, Pakistan, Brazil, Italy and many more) overt bribery is considered perfectly ok, and quite right too. Wherever the Sissies have got a grip (the US, UK, France, Germany, Scandinavia, Japan to name but a few), it is rather more ticklish to enter into this kind of thing. But if you can't bribe, you can still polish up ego, remind them of how fantastic they are and laugh in all the right places.

It is important to never show weakness, this is a truism of Terribleness. However, it can actually help to ask your boss's opinion, i.e. for their help from time to time. Best to stick to stuff you feel extremely confident about when asking for the boss's help. This way you can have an insightful, intelligent conversation where almost certainly the boss will learn a thing or two. The effect is that the boss walks away thinking, "If they asked for help on that, they must be brilliant at the rest...".

Invite the boss to dinner at your house if you get on particularly well, perhaps even on skiing holidays or something similar if families are at similar stages and it seems natural enough. Remember, they hold the trigger on your next promotion — so treat them with the respect and deference they deserve. It means that they will have a very different view of you than everyone else, who will see the true tyrant you really are. This is fine for as long as they are your boss. The moment they cease to be your boss, it is best to try and organise for them to leave the organisation one way or the other. They can become a dangerous source of rumour about your pleasant, sunny disposition. This cannot be tolerated and, like a cuckoo ousting smaller siblings from the nest, do exactly the same if you ever get the chance.

It is almost 2.30pm by the time Gordon gets back to his office. He spends thirty minutes with his secretary going through emails and various communications. At 3pm Mike, his press secretary who received the random rant at 5am, comes to see him. Mike is visibly upset and nervous. Gordon does nothing to alleviate these symptoms of distress, knowing that even the slightest show of weakness or conciliation now will destroy all the hard work he has done so far today. Mike is a solid performer, perhaps not the best press secretary there has ever been, but he handles the external communications issues of the department with diligence, accuracy and purpose. Gordon has come to trust and rely on him, but knows that this is no excuse to go soft.

Mike sits down and smiles nervously before asking if there has been a specific incident or lapse that Gordon is particularly worried about because he can't remember having messed up for all the time they have worked together. Gordon knows not to fall into this trap and responds instead by asking a series of questions:

- How long have we worked together?
- What is Mike looking to achieve in his career?
- How would he describe the nature of the relationship between a head of department and their press secretary?
- What would be his ideal pet? (Gordon must have read this book and flinches visibly when Mike says he'd like a kitten.)

Mike is on the back foot. He's not sure where this is going and some of the questions are simply obscure. At around 3.30, he senses the meeting is beginning to draw to an end and still nothing specific has been mentioned. Gordon asks him to get something ready for a brief radio appearance he is due to give tomorrow morning and pushes his chair back, suggesting a definite end to the meeting. Mike is elated and very relieved. Perhaps this is going to go ok after all. Just as he is about to leave, Gordon says, "Let's just be sure we are not having this conversation again." "No, absolutely not... errr... thanks," Mike ventures. He has a strange sense of having dodged an invisible bullet. It is far from clear as to what has caused Gordon's displeasure, although there is no doubting Gordon is displeased with him. So he must have done, or not done, something. Clearly, he will need to re-double his efforts and decides immediately to get in touch with his peers in other departments to compare notes, just to see if there is anything he is missing. Maybe putting in a few more hours wouldn't be a bad idea either...

In Chapter 2, we looked at the ideal conditions for Terribleness to flourish. One of those was uncertainty and here Gordon is driving Mike's experience of uncertainty to considerable levels. Mike is clear that Gordon is unhappy but has no idea about what. When he questions this, all he seems to achieve is to irritate Gordon further, so he desists. The lesson we can all apply here from Gordon's exemplary behaviour is to remember that it is our job as leaders to drive the performance of our people. This is sometimes best achieved by using their existing level of performance as an example of what you don't want to see. This may generate questions around specificity, but don't get drawn into detail — it is your job to remain strategic. Gordon keeps criticism and feedback as high level as possible, generating a sense of mystery around the desired level of performance. This is then an opportunity for the employee to go away and figure it out for themselves. This is particularly helpful if you are not entirely clear as to the precise nature of the role of all

> Keep criticism and feedback as high level as possible, generating a sense of mystery around the desired level of performance.

the people that report to you. As you become more Terrible, and correspondingly more senior in the organisation, you will increasingly find people reporting to you that you have no idea what they do. This makes micro-management difficult, so you may need to turn to other approaches in order to drive performance to a satisfactory level. This is a highly effective, efficient and not to mention professional way of managing performance. You don't need to mess about with forms and annual reviews if you are as proficient as Gordon.

Gordon now has a few minutes to prepare for Sue's appearance at 4pm to talk about inter-departmental cooperation. He is dreading this meeting so asks a passing minion to go and make him a coffee with two sugars in order to bolster his energy. He asks a couple of direct reports to stand in his office for a moment to get some details about the real opportunities and obstacles to collaborating with Sue's department, plus some stories about how specific people in her department have been obstructive in the past.

Sue arrives and is ushered into his office. The meeting progresses bumpily. Sue is keen to create a unit comprising members of staff from both departments to act as a joint service centre for data analysis and reporting in order to save money, time and generate common reporting standards in what she claims are two very similar disciplines. Gordon is not fooled, and can see that she is simply trying to fob off her low-value report writing to his department — who obviously do it better than her lot. OR, alternatively, she is trying to build her empire by stealing away his valued data analytics team. He's not sure exactly which one of these is her exact motive but he is convinced it is one of these, and whichever one it is, he knows that Sue will get what she wants over his dead body.

Accordingly, he digs in with lots of general pleasantries and a lot of distracting gossip about other heads of department. He then states some of the specific instances of poor cooperation people in his department have experienced at the hands of her people. Gordon, being meticulous, is sure to mention the specific names and the dates of the instances where he has them. He then rounds up by talking generally about some of the wider aims of his department, i.e. those areas that make it sound as though their areas of concern have least overlap. At about 5pm, Sue leaves dejected and browbeaten and thoroughly unconvinced that a collaborative effort between their departments is ever going to happen. Gordon sees her to the reception area and, as she leaves, he waits for her to be safely out of earshot before turning to the receptionist, winking conspiratorially and saying, "I really hate that woman".

Before we look at the broader lessons from this episode in Gordon's day, take note of the detail right at the beginning — the coffee. Gordon knows that it's important to involve every member of staff in supporting his leadership, and he understands the thrill they will experience if they are singled out to make his coffee. If they are a relatively senior minion, it may be an irritating thrill admittedly, but it gives them an opportunity to off-load the task on an even more lowly minion.

Never just make your own coffee — use every opportunity to be Terrible, no matter how trivial. Next, he is faced with obvious competition from another department.

The first lesson here is to see collaboration for what it really is. Ask yourself, "Who really wants to collaborate?" Right. No one does, and neither do you, so don't be fooled. Of course, you have to go along with the whole charade of pretending to listen and be interested and save overheads and blah blah blah. But, never ever take your eye off the fact that this is an opportunity to demonstrate your true Terrible nature and, at the same time, a risk of losing territory. Gordon responds in just the right way, with a combination of distraction, aggression and confusion. Einstein said, "If you can't convince them, confuse them", or something to that effect. I tend to think that even when you can convince them, it isn't a bad idea to loop back and confuse them at the end. In business, if you are confused, what do you do? That's right, you nod and try to look intelligent while secretly worrying that the other person must either be a lot more intelligent than you are (unlikely obviously, but you are prepared to dally with the idea), or that they must have a much better grasp of the topic and its complex nuances than you do (more likely). However people respond to confusion, it never hurts the Terrible leader to spread it around. Confusion and uncertainty go hand in hand, and we know how much a good Terrible leader likes uncertainty.

> Never just make your own coffee — use every opportunity to be Terrible, no matter how trivial.

Now, if we know anything about Gordon by now, it is that he never misses an opportunity for Terribleness. Notice how he meticulously mentions the specific names of the people who have caused problems. This gives Sue ammunition with which to return to her department. Alternatively, if Sue is a Sissy leader, it gives her a dilemma as to what to do with the information — which, in many ways, is even better. We will talk in subsequent chapters about the importance of establishing a blame culture, and here Gordon gives us just a little indication about how it is best done. Dropping names associated with unsuccessful projects is a subtle way of pinning the blame to the specific miscreants you want to demonise. A simple way of remembering how and when to pin blame (and we'll come back to this) goes as follows:

- If it went well — I did it.
- If it went ok — I did it, despite the limitations of the morons I am forced to have working for me.
- If it went badly — it was the morons.

In this way, you can help your boss to understand the causality of success and failure in your area. This is an important part of root cause analysis and operational excellence — your manager will want to ascertain cause and effect if things have gone wrong. It is at precisely this point you need to be able to point quickly and clearly to the HR manager. You can always blame them for having

> Dropping names associated with unsuccessful projects is a subtle way of pinning the blame to the specific miscreants you want to demonise.

hired a load of pond-dwelling mentally deficient youths, you know, the ones with one leg longer than the other. Look around you now, they are probably wearing checked shirts.

It's 5pm, Gordon's favourite time of the day. The real slackers in his office are beginning to think about going home. Gordon doesn't normally finish up until around 8pm, so in his mind, neither should anyone else. Of course, in reality, they do start to escape in seriously large numbers from about 6.30pm, but only to his constant chagrin. To counter that, as he walks back towards his office, he takes a detour through some of the administrative departments and engages a couple of shift leaders in some general discussion about targets and call volumes. Someone nervously starts turning off their computer and putting personal effects into a rucksack. They are on the far side of the office and foolishly think they will escape detection; they are in between Gordon and the exit, and if they can just sidle out of the door without being noticed, perhaps walking just in front of the post room guy with his trolley.... "YOU THERE!" bellows Gordon, "WHERE DO YOU THINK YOU'RE GOING?". They hadn't even made it five steps from their desk. Gordon commands them to go to his office and wait there, finds out who his manager is and drags them with him back to his lair. After 15 minutes of berating, banging and shouting, the slacker and his manager re-appear from Gordon's office and head back to their desks. No one attempts to leave until 6.40pm that night...

Gordon now spends the most productive part of his day catching up on emails, writing some communications and working through his diary for the next day's appointments (which naturally he moves around mercilessly). He tries wherever possible to keep his emails to one-liners, ideally just using the subject field. This way he is able to read and churn out over 100 emails in the short period between around 5.15pm and 7.30pm. At 7.30, he calls for a taxi (his secretary has gone home) and has them pick him up in 10 minutes. Most people have gone home, although obviously the Finance team are still slogging away. On his way out, Gordon passes a pizza delivery man coming into reception.

A useful habit to get yourself into is brief emails. Gordon knows that his time is precious. He never bothers with niceties. Research has found that if you put together all the time you spend typing, 'please' and 'thank you' and 'kind regards' and 'it was good to see you' and blah blah blah, it comes to around 43 hours every week for the average leader. You are not an average leader, you are a Terrible leader, and as such, you can short-circuit the whole dreary obligation of asking after people's weekends and providing 'context'. You can actually trim things right down, as you will see below from a series of example emails used by some of the best Terrible leaders in the business. If Stalin could have sent emails, they might have read along the following lines:

- By Wednesday 3pm latest.
- Very disappointing.
- No.
- Not your remit.

- Re-write whole report.
- Unacceptable.
- Not relevant.
- Understood.
- Ok.
- You're asking the wrong question.
- Not a priority.

> You are a Terrible leader, and as such, you can short-circuit the whole dreary obligation of asking after people's weekends.

None of these emails takes more than a second or two to type. They are succinct and to the point, and in modern business, we need more leaders able to express themselves in these terms. Things move fast, workloads increase and leaders need to be able to cut through. Yes, your people will want all of that nice, soft 'how are you' stuff. This is because they are essentially spineless. You, on the other hand, are busy, going places and ambitious. Oh, and you have a spine.

It is also important to be authentic (we agree with the Sissy leaders on this point). Asking after someone's health, or family, or (even worse) their pets would suggest you actually care. This is non-authentic behaviour and should be discouraged. Unless, of course, you are concerned their ill-health may prevent them from conducting their duties effectively, in which case it is wise to check. HR might have a policy about this, but generally if they've had a stroke and can't be trusted with a photocopier in case it sets something

> Your people will want all of that nice, soft 'how are you' stuff. This is because they are essentially spineless.

off, then it's pretty safe, and thoroughly advisable to sack them. I mean, who wants sick or messed-up people hanging around leeching money from the company?

It's 8.30pm and Gordon walks through his front door. The kids are asleep and his wife is just putting the finishing touches to his evening meal. He admonishes her appropriately for a lack of variety of vegetables before settling to his meal and a chat about their respective days. He finds out she has had some trouble with the school about getting little Oliver the instrument he wanted to play in the school band, and Gordon takes a note to call the headmaster in the morning and wonders fleetingly if he could add her to his early morning rant list. The dry-cleaners have done an exemplary job with his suits after he threatened legal proceedings after the last debacle. He tells his wife about imminent promotions '*although nothing is definite yet*' and shares a joke about his spineless and useless boss. At 9.30pm, he takes the dog out for a walk while his wife cleans up after dinner and at 10pm, he kisses the children good night, makes cocoa for him and a camomile tea for her and they retire to the bedroom to read. The light goes out and all is calm. The curtains suck gently back and forth in the window frame and only a faint police siren and an occasional passing car breaks the silence.

Gordon is now asleep and dreaming of dragons and princesses. In this one day, he has brought to focus 20 lessons that we can apply to our day-to-day efforts to become more Terrible. Let's recap.

Chapter Five — Lessons in Terrible

1. Manage the conditions of your terribleness — trip yourself up from time to time, get out on the wrong side of bed.
2. Make Terribleness a routine, schedule early morning rants to drive high performance...
3. ...but remember to be flexible and take the opportunities to be Terrible whenever they present themselves.
4. Complain a lot, and wherever possible, unreasonably.
5. Manage your diary carefully, move people around at the last minute and catch other people unprepared.
6. Walk the floor (or 'management by walking around' as the Sissies call it) and terrorise people as you go.
7. Never remember people's names, even when you do.
8. Ask people difficult questions at random times and show obvious disapproval when they struggle to answer.
9. Manage people's expectations, i.e. make sure they never get what they expect, keep them guessing and in a constant state of uncertainty.
10. Tear down others' arguments rather than building up your own.
11. Turn up late and leave early.
12. Make the boss like you (but stab them in the back at the first opportunity).

Chapter Five — Lessons in Terrible

13. Generate uncertainty around expected performance levels.
14. Never give specific feedback, except sometimes. But maybe not. Or...
15. Be suspicious of people who want to collaborate.
16. Confuse and distract whenever possible.
17. Work to create a culture of blame.
18. Shout at people who leave early.
19. Send very brief emails.
20. Get rid of sick people.

Now, if in Chapter 4 you scored quite low on the Terribleness Quotient instrument, it might be a little unreasonable to expect to put all these hints and tips into action at once. Instead, take one or two and try and make them a habit. Over a period of months and years, you will find that it gets easier and easier. In the next few chapters, we will dig into a little more detail around how you can express your Terribleness fully. We will look at the theory as well as the practice and take our understanding of true Terribleness still further. But, for the moment, we will take leave of our (totally fictitious, not based on anybody) hero: Gordon the Terrible. May his reign be golden and his Terribleness legendary. For us, it is time to return, bleary-eyed but buoyed by his positive example, to reality...

CHAPTER 6
AUTHENTIC TYRANNY

In our previous chapter, we used an exemplar of Terribleness to learn how we can pepper our daily lives with Terrible deeds and actions. Some of you will have read Chapter 5 and thought, "Excellent, I'll take some notes, and perhaps I could try this or that on Monday". Others will have read the chapter and thought, "That's just not going to work for me". The problem is, if you have not already established a reputation and image as a Terrible leader, it might be hard to suddenly start throwing office furniture around and calling everyone reprobates. Let me illustrate this with a story from my childhood that I'm sure will resonate for everyone.

I went to an all-boys' school. Ok, so this story might not resonate for everyone after all... At this school, like at all other schools, there were teachers that could instil fear, respect and apprehension at their mere arrival in the classroom. Imagine trying to keep a room of thirty 15-year-old boys quiet, focused and disciplined for an hour at a time. It must have been next to impossible, but these teachers not only did it, they did it with ease. We were genuinely worried about what they would do to us should we step out of line. Shouting was the least we could expect; at worst, we could expect detentions, a visit to the headmaster, mild physical intimidation, or some inappropriate touching. Basically we could expect the sort of things that could make a 15-year-old boy's day go from good to downright awful if we gave them even half a reason for doing so. A loud cough would be enough. A rustled sweet wrapper would spell detention for a week. One boy was given detention for a month for wearing an elaborate dental brace that a teacher mistook for a Walkman.

These teachers were Terrible to the core. In their spare time, they didn't go on long walks, prune bonsai trees or build papier-mâché reconstructions of the bridge over the river Kwai. Not at all. In their spare time, they terrorised more children at local boy scout clubs or church Sunday schools. Their classroom Terribleness was not an act, it was an authentic reality. It was just who they were, and who they preferred to be. When they weren't in the classroom, they felt itchy and awkward, so they took up hobbies that allowed them to express more Terribleness elsewhere. They probably dreamed Terrible dreams where more fanatical forms of child punishment were permitted, or even encouraged at the school.

Then there were other teachers. They wanted us to respect them, but I suspect, not as much as they wanted us to *like* them. For them, classroom discipline was a complete nightmare. Their desire to be popular meant that they were never keen to send anyone to the headmaster, far less were they likely to actively watch for opportunities and excuses to do so. Now, occasionally, we would get the upper hand on these teachers, cause a complete ruckus and send them running from the room in despair. Senior teachers would intervene, the boys would all claim plausible deniability and the class would be disbanded for the morning or the afternoon, parents called and the weakened teacher given some stern talking-to by the headmaster about classroom discipline and control. The very next lesson, they would be tougher, much tougher. But this toughness was not of the same sort that the authentically terrifying teachers had. It was a fake toughness, born of necessity rather than pleasure. It neither scared us nor changed our behaviour. This was my first lesson in what it meant to be authentically Terrible. You have to be authentic through and through, it can't be an act or a style you adopt for nine hours a day. You have to be the real thing. And if you can't, you'll never be a Terrible leader because we can all spot when you're pretending. When an actor acts, we can tell. When someone is lying, we can (for the most part) tell. But what if you're only partially down the road to full authentic Terribleness? How can you start to signal your authenticity before it is fully formed? Does this even work?

> You have to be authentic through and through, it can't be an act or a style you adopt for nine hours a day.

This is one of very few areas where Terrible leadership and Sissy leadership writing and thinking overlap considerably. In the Sissy management development literature, you will find a lot of talk about authentic leadership. One of the Sissiest and most puke-inducing is by Goffee and Jones called, *Why Should Anyone Be Led By You?* Now, obviously, they're writing about becoming an authentic Sissy leader, which would be a Terrible mistake, and therefore all their advice and writing is topsy-turvy, muddled and round the wrong way. It's all about personal disclosure, communication and managing social distance. There are probably pictures of puppies and pixies and the sort if you read it cover to cover. We don't want to end up like this at all, but they do have a point. If you don't sound, act and behave Terrible, *consistently*, people simply won't respond appropriately to your Terribleness.

Two leaders, one authentically Terrible and one just going through the motions, saying and doing precisely the same things, at the same time, won't have the same impact. The followers of the non-authentic, inner Sissy leader will know they can afford to ignore their well-honed acts of Terribleness. A well-crafted rant will be passed off as 'just their way when they get a bit annoyed'. The threat to move a particularly useless minion to some outpost of a project in a dead-end department will be interpreted as, 'just a flash in the pan — they'll never actually do it'. Can you think of anything worse? A Terrible leader that wasn't taken seriously? If that sounds like you, then go hang your head in shame. Take a long walk on a cold day without your jacket and think long and hard about what you have done. People like you give all of Terrible leadership a bad name.

Terrible leadership is not just about ranting, waving your arms around and handing out brutal punishments arbitrarily. It is only 90% about these things. It is also about pushing people in a personally unsustainable way to achieve staggering results and then finding out ways of personally benefitting from these efforts far beyond the scale of your pay packet. So, if you want to be a truly Terrible leader, you need to be authentic, otherwise people are just going to ignore you. To achieve this, you need to follow a few simple rules:

> Terrible leadership is not just about ranting, waving your arms around and handing out brutal punishments arbitrarily. It is only 90% about these things.

1. Never show *any* weaknesses.

Darth Vader in *Star Wars* didn't disclose a discomfort with doing technical presentations about the Death Star. Ferdinand Marcos didn't own up to a tendency to misplace government funds. Genghis Khan didn't confess to an inability to match soft furnishings. Similarly, you should never show any weakness. Terrible leaders at their most impressive are better than us at everything — they inspire awe and dread in equal proportion. Now, of course, you will not be perfect and you may have a few gaps in your list of awesome capabilities. Here are a few common leadership gaps you may or may not have:

- Poor planning skills.
- Lack of strategic insight.
- Inability to influence senior stakeholders.
- Low intelligence.
- Poor personal hygiene.

Obviously, none of these is a big issue in any real sense and none of these prevents you from being a truly great Terrible leader. But, should any of your minions find out that you have these or other weaknesses, you need to take action fast. You need to silence them, either by having them killed (e.g. they might need to accidentally fall inside the waste compactor), sacked or, ideally, both (be sure to sack them first). You will then appear impermeable, impenetrable and impervious to all those who behold you.

2. Never let people get to know the *real* you. Unless you want to frighten them.

Let's go back to the Death Star. We walk into Darth Vader's office. What do you imagine you will see? Pictures of his friends and family? A colourful stress ball or two? Some mindless quotes about the importance of innovation under the picture of a snowy mountain? A squash racket? Of course not. It will be sparse and minimalist; perhaps just a box of light-sabre wipes and a helmet duster. Nothing will be on display that would give away a passion for newts, or a predilection for cycling, or membership of a football supporter's club (incidentally, Vader supported the Yankees, but the only Death Star employee who accidentally found this out, a technician called Gareth Jenkins, was light-sabred to death in a most unpleasant way).

To your minions, you need to remain aloof, unknown and feared. It is hard to fear someone if you know they collect old Barbie dolls or if you know they like to leave early on Wednesdays to do life modelling at the local art college. So, remove all trappings of your personal life from your workplace. At no cost engage in mindless chit-chat about families, children, hobbies or pastimes. To your feckless employees, your whole reason for being should be to put the fear of god into them for every one of their miserable, pointless and futile waking hours. There should be no distraction, and while you can have a hobby, no one at work more junior than you should know about it.

There is only one exception to this rule: generating fear. If you feel a minion has become a bit uppity or lacks the right level of spine-tingling fear and respect for you, it is permissible to divulge a small detail about your personal life (it doesn't have to be true) that you feel will instil that sense of awe and dread. For example, you might let slip that, on the previous evening, you personally castrated your Rottweiler to save on vet's fees. Or you might mention that your opponent in the weekend's Karate bout ended up in hospital and will only ever eat through a straw for the rest of their lives. You might recall how you slapped your child's teacher when they complained about you booing at the school play, or you might recall fondly how you threw away all your children's toys when they failed to tidy them up within the strict five-minute limit you had set them. If this doesn't work, try recounting how you had so much fun ruining the careers of a few of your previous employees at your previous company.

3. Go out of your way to remind your staff that they are pond scum.

Your people may initially believe that they have some things in common with you. It is important that they realise, and realise quickly, that this is not the case. Remember, you were selected to be the boss, so you are intellectually, physically, socially, morally and in all other ways ending in '–ly' superior to them. Your staff will appreciate it if you can find the small ways to reinforce this point. The coffee machine they use will not be sufficient for your executive needs, so have a better one installed next to it and make it clear that if anyone is found using it other than you, they will be flayed alive. Unless they're making coffee for you, in which case if they use the old machine, they will be flayed alive. If you can't tell which machine they've used when they bring back the coffee then flay them alive just in case and get rid of the better machine and replace it with an even better one so that the difference is really obvious. You'll need to do this every few months or so as your executive taste buds become accustomed to the good coffee.

> You are intellectually, physically, socially, morally and in all other ways ending in '–ly' superior to them.

Make sure you have parking privileges and that a sign in the car park makes it clear that you have them. Have a big, luxurious office with beautiful potted plants, leather armchairs, a recessed plasma screen, private bathroom — basically if you can think of it, get it. Not because you want it — not at all, but because it serves as a reminder to your hapless employees that *you are better than them*. They'll appreciate this as it will build in them a strengthened sense of belief in you, your decisions and your capability. And people like to be confident in their boss, so really, you're only doing it for them.

4. Create an environment of high risk and low support for everyone, except you.

Obviously, you want to create an environment of low risk and high support for yourself, but it should be precisely the other way around for your staff. Authentic Terrible leaders create high risk environments for their people so that success is met with suspicion and re-allocation to more peripheral projects and failure with a horse whip. If someone does well in your team, you need to be wary of them (see Chapters 7 and 8). They might be trying to get your job. Think about where you can assign them to ensure future success is highly unlikely. For this purpose,

> Terrible leaders create high risk environments for their people so that success is met with suspicion and re-allocation to more peripheral projects.

it is helpful if you can hold back a couple of particularly poisonous, career-ruining secondments. Anything to do with change and IT normally does the trick. Equally, if someone is struggling you should aim to create the equivalent sensation of free-fall; that sensation of terminal velocity, impending death, fear and loss of sphincter control. Avoid talking with them and discourage others from talking to them. Pile more demands on them and ask them to work faster. Undermine their competence with key stakeholders and tut when you walk past their desk.

If you can follow that four-point plan, your Terribleness will soon be viewed from far and wide as truly authentic. People will believe in your Terrible intentions and will therefore behave accordingly. A good way to gauge if you have become authentically Terrible is how much you enjoy a random act of Terribleness. To track your level of authenticity, it is a good idea to create a measurement system for yourself. Write down on a piece of paper a list of the things you most enjoy doing. Try and think of the non-Terrible things that give you the greatest pleasure. On a typical list you might find:

- Breaking the seal on a fresh jar of instant coffee.
- Throwing a piece of scrunched up paper straight into the bin/trash.
- Running late for the train, but catching it anyway because it's running late too.
- Cracking open the perfect boiled egg.
- The smell of freshly-mown grass.
- Fresh snow in the park with no one's footprints.
- The smell of fresh linen on the bed.

You know the kind of stuff — the stuff that just makes you happy. Now, try and get these in some sort of order. Which ones would you fight for the most to keep? Once you have rank ordered them, you have in your hands a sort of happiness scale. Near the top is mega-happiness and near the bottom is deep contentment.

Once you've got your happiness scale sorted out, we need to fix on a random act of Terribleness. Some good ones include:

- Hurling abuse at a minion for no good reason.
- Deliberately throwing coffee over a member of staff.

- Responding to an email with, 'You're an idiot'.
- Moving a highly-performing member of staff off a high-profile project for no good reason.
- Asking a small team to work late in order to meet you in the evening, and then cancelling the meeting at the last minute.

It doesn't really matter what you choose, just try and make sure it is discrete, easy and fun to do, and something you can repeat over and over. Every three months or so, carry out this random act of Terribleness and get out your happiness chart. Where on your happiness chart would you place it? As your Terribleness unfurls and grows, you may find it initially sits at the bottom of the chart, like eating a mince pie (a strange English culinary Christmas pie made with dried fruit — weird) that actually tastes ok rather than rancid. But, in time, as your Terribleness takes hold and is carefully nurtured, hopefully, you will find that you rank this act of Terribleness much higher. Eventually you will find that the smell of freshly-baked bread is nothing in comparison to the sound a stapler makes as it collides fleshily with the skull of a junior minion. And when this is true and you find yourself going out of your way to create opportunities for Terribleness, then the authenticity question has answered itself. You won't just be Terrible on the outside; you will be Terrible to the core.

Chapter Six — Lessons in Terrible

- There is a difference between inner Terribleness and expressed Terribleness. The ideal state is to fuel the latter with the former, but this takes time and discipline to achieve.
- Authentic Terribleness is when you no longer act Terribly consciously, you do it because that's just how you do it...
- ...and because you like it.
- Never show any weakness. Your staff must perceive you to be better than them at everything.
- Never let your staff get to know the real you. Remain aloof and mysterious, unless you want to frighten them.
- Remind your staff that they are pond scum. Invest in all the small signals that remind them of their inferiority, such as a nice office and lush pot plants for you, and cheap, second-hand chairs for them.
- Create a climate of high risk and low support for your people. If people do well, banish them. If people do badly, pressurise them. The ones that scrape along, just leave them alone and they'll be grateful.
- Measure how much you enjoy random acts of Terribleness to track your level of authenticity.

The best Terrible leaders don't act Terrible.
They *are* Terrible.

part three
Terrible
team leaders

Let's take another break from being Terrible again. In a moment, the Terrible leader sallies forth to do the unspeakable to their team. But, for the moment, let's just reflect on what we can learn about our relationship with leadership from the previous three chapters.

Chapter 4 is plain daft on one level (so if you bought a leopard I do hope you kept the receipt). But, on another level, it is deadly serious. You need to develop your level of awareness as to your innate strengths and weaknesses as a leader. We were all born left or right-handed, or a mixture of both. In the same way some of us were born handed for aspects of leadership, and not for others. It doesn't really matter, in the same way it doesn't really matter if you are left or right-handed, but it is extremely useful to understand which way you're wired. For example, some of us are naturally interested in what happens next, tomorrow, in the far off distant future. Some of us just aren't. But leadership is (for the most part) a future-oriented role, your people can take care of the here and now. Understanding your own tendency will help you to manage yourself. So, get yourself online and find a good, reputable company who can launch you on a leadership psychometric and get some feedback.

Chapter 5 is absolutely full of wonderful reversible advice. Most of the 20 lessons can literally be switched over, e.g. Lesson 10: Tear down others' arguments rather than building up your own. Simply know that by far the most effective way to influence others is to fully explore their proposal, see the merit in it, and find ways of connecting what they are trying to achieve with your proposal, i.e. do exactly the opposite. Don't get rid of sick people (Lesson 20), adapt to allow and encourage them to contribute fully. Don't walk the floor to terrorise people (Lesson 6), instead walk the floor to encourage and support people. The one I just want to pause over is Lesson 12: Make the boss like you (but stab them in the back at the first opportunity). Now, obviously, you don't go about stabbing your boss in the back. Instead, find ways of talking positively about their influence and impact. But, it is important to develop a fruitful relationship with your boss. The key to this lesson is in the words 'make' and 'like'. You can't make your boss like you. You should make an effort to get to know and earn the trust of your boss and all of your colleagues equally. If that turns into 'liking' then great.

The lessons in Chapter 6 are actually rather subtle and hard to live with if you are naturally a private person. Disclosing things about your personal life can, for some, feel unprofessional. The Terrible leader's approach of showing no weakness and disclosing nothing about their personal life might appeal. But here's the thing: we trust the people we know. And when we trust someone, we feel safe putting ourselves in a vulnerable position, believing that they will behave in accordance with our best interests. In a work context, this translates into working really hard. Our people will only work really hard for us if they trust that we won't snigger 'suckers' behind their backs, and take the credit for their hard work. It has been calculated that people will generate up to 48% more output when they feel a strong sense of trust in their employer and engagement with their work. So, earning their trust is a passport to your success, and you'll never accomplish that if you present yourself as aloof and without flaw. In other words, you share your weaknesses and the 'real you' with them, they see you're not some aloof know-it-all and they work hard safe in the knowledge that you'll give them all the credit you can.

There are also important lessons in Chapter 6 about the symbolic importance of lessening the perceived gaps between levels in the organisation. The senior leader who abandons their plush corner office, converts it into a meeting room and gets out onto the floor in the open-plan working area with everyone goes a long way to saying, 'we're in this together'. As leaders, we should be approachable and normal, judged by our actions, not the symbolic representations of our status. Finally, it is important to create an environment that balances risk and challenge with support, rather than the Terrible approach of creating high risk with low support! This is especially true if your team needs to develop innovative new products, approaches, services etc. If they are engaged in solving tough problems, they need to be supported to take risks, which loops us right back to Chapter 3 and our reversed lesson from Vlad the Impaler: treat mistakes (the right, non-stupid kind) as an opportunity to learn and congratulate people for pushing themselves.

As you grow as a leader, my hope for you is that you can begin a dialogue with yourself. Not the early onset signs of dementia, I mean a reflective conversation between the you that doesn't lead and the you that does. These two voices will merge with time, but for the moment, it is useful if you can stand back from time to time and think about what it is like to be led by you. If you're not sure what it's like, then you can always ask those lucky enough to actually have that experience, which leads us nicely to part three of this book: your leadership and others. Now, let's go and see what the Terrible leader is up to...

CHAPTER 7
MAKING THEM MISERABLE

So far, we have focused on Terribleness and you. The rest of this book now turns to look at how you can inflict your Terribleness on others, and we start by looking at those in the best position to appreciate your new-found tyrannical tendencies: your team. These are the people that give you the most problems today, in all probability. They are the people who look to you for leadership and they are the people whose performance will largely dictate your own success and fortunes. They are inferior to you, not just in terms of personal wealth and intelligence, but also in terms of their stature and importance within the organisation. You may have many thousands of people under you, you may just have one, and in the following three chapters, we will look at how to lead and manage them according to Terrible principles.

The most important lesson you will ever learn in leadership is that the greatest threat to your future career, Terrible or otherwise, comes from those you manage. Yes, it's those pesky minions of yours that amount to your greatest challenge. Finding this hard to believe, that a bunch of individuals with a shared brain the size of a walnut could depose you? That's understandable, but consider this: leaders only ever move on because of very few reasons:

1. **They die:** this can be from natural causes, in which case you are most likely to be retired, so this shouldn't be an issue unless you've been feeling under the weather recently. But you can also catch death as a result of poisoning or other team member activities, so it is worth being circumspect about receiving gifts of food.

2. **They move up:** this is the way you want to move on, as it means you have succeeded in achieving sufficient levels of Terribleness to warrant a promotion.

3. **They are deposed:** i.e. they are sacked, sidelined, replaced or asked to leave. This is the most common reason for moving on. Think about it, there are fewer and fewer leadership roles the further up the organisation you go, so therefore, necessarily, most leaders don't make it and are deposed. And who deposes them? Their boss. Wrong! Their boss has nothing to gain by getting rid of a minion unless they suspected them of plotting against them, which, being Terrible, you would never let them suspect for a moment (although obviously you will be plotting). No, the deposing is done by your subordinates. Not overtly, obviously, they don't have the intelligence or the power to bring about your demise openly. But they can scheme, plot, undermine and cast aspersions until your name is mud across the organisation.

I want you to think about your team members right now, try and picture their faces. They might be smiling, nodding approvingly and gratefully or looking up to you in admiration and respect. It seems hard to believe that amongst them is your own personal Brutus, your Judas. But there it is, statistically, it is very probably the case. You need to wake up and see them for the threat they are. Just because they have the collective drive, intelligence and wit of a swarm of jellyfish doesn't make them any less dangerous. Terrible leaders, unlike their Sissy counterparts, are alert to this and manage the risks accordingly. Risk management is about identification, quantification and mitigation. Hopefully, you will begin to become aware of the risk. You will see that it is always the biggest single risk to your future success and now we can move towards mitigation. In a strange way, it is possible that Sissy leaders are subconsciously aware of the risk too but they have a completely different approach to mitigation. Before we look at the correct, sensible, Terrible approach, let's just take a minute for some light brevity and look at the Sissy approach.

> The greatest threat to your future career, Terrible or otherwise, comes from those you manage.

Sissy leaders, in order to prevent people from stabbing them mercilessly in the back at the earliest opportunity, attempt to become friends with their direct reports. They will get to know them, trying to understand their career aspirations, their hopes and fears. They will try to demonstrate they care about them and they will try and further their career for them by supplying them with developmental opportunities. They will spend time working through their objectives, providing them with clear, unambiguous goals and they will even carry the can if their people do dumb stuff. They try to create a 'culture of trust and empowerment'.

It's incredible isn't it — so much wasted effort! Let's use Terrible logic to unpick this approach straight away. First off, the notion of becoming friends with your employees. We know this is a foolish strategy because if any of your employees have any Terrible tendencies (and this book can fall into anyone's hands, unfortunately) then they will take advantage of this approach straightaway. They will let you believe that they are your best buddy and then haul you over hot coals just as soon as their bonus isn't quite what they expected. Also, being someone's friend takes time and effort. You are here to get promoted and make money. Ask yourself this, how does making friends with your direct reports get you promoted or more money? Right! It doesn't, so don't do it!

Secondly, this idea of getting to know their career aspirations and hopes. If they're honest (and most of them probably aren't), they aspire to your job. In their puny and dishevelled minds, they believe they can do it better than you do. Some will tell you this outright. This is an obvious case of insubordination, and if flogging is permissible in your company's code of conduct, I'd suggest you start there. Check with HR first though, because sometimes it's better just to sack them. Most of them won't be this brazen though, but once again, don't be fooled, just because they say they don't want your job doesn't mean to say they don't. They're just being sly.

On this point, you can break your direct reports down into four distinct groups:

Group 1
Want your job and they say they do (typically no more than 5% of the workforce).
Appropriate management response: Flogging or immediate dismissal (check with local HR policies).

Group 2
Want your job but say they don't (around 70% of the workforce).
Appropriate management response: keep on top of them, wear them down, prevent them from ever believing they're good enough (see below for hints and tips).

Group 3
Don't know what they want (around 20% of the workforce).
Appropriate management response: generally abuse — they won't put up much of a fight (see Chapter 9 for some ideas). This gives them something to focus on and can be rewarding for you and the organisation.

Group 4
Genuinely happy in their role, no aspirations to progress (very rare, less than 5%).
Appropriate management response: deep cynicism for a start, remember these are extremely rare, like snow leopards. To carry

on with the metaphor, are you sure you haven't just got an over-fed cat on your hands? To continue further with the metaphor, if you're convinced it is a real snow leopard then do the obvious and right thing. Shoot it, skin it and hang it as a trophy on your office wall. Ok, the metaphor breaks down a little here, but essentially, don't trust this group. Their motivations are strange and alien and their behaviour very hard to predict. Try and move them to another department where they will cause trouble for someone else.

So as you can see, 'research' shows that around 70% of your direct reports are essentially plotting to get your job. This might feel a little alarming and I'm sorry if this dawning realisation leaves you feeling a little queasy. But please don't panic. Panicking is not seemly and it certainly isn't Terrible. Help is at hand and in this chapter, we will walk through a series of tried and tested approaches for keeping your treacherous direct reports at bay. We will look at a Terrible leadership model called the 4E

> 'Research' shows that around 70% of your direct reports are essentially plotting to get your job.

model. 4E stands for empowerment, empathy, engagement and energy. Your job is to keep these all as low as possible as the higher the readings for any of these, the more likely a coup is brewing. Making them miserable (the title of this chapter) is not a tongue-in-cheek throwaway comment, it is a management mantra that if taken to heart, will ensure your longevity in your current role, and your uncontested march to the next one.

The 4E model of Terrible leadership

Empowerment

Let's take a look at the first of our four Es. Empowerment is a complex concept. Firstly, note the word in the middle of the word em***power***ment. Power is obviously something you don't want your direct reports to have. The remaining em-ment doesn't sound too dangerous, but it's probably best to be on the safe side and prevent them from having any of that too. For a person to be empowered, it typically involves three things:

1. They are clear about what they are accountable for and clear that they have permission to pursue any line of action they deem sensible to achieve those accountabilities.
2. They have the necessary skills and competencies to achieve that task.
3. They have the self-belief and confidence that they can act in order to achieve the task in front of them.

Just breaking empowerment down like this into its constituent parts should begin to waft the scent of opportunity towards your Terrible nostrils. We touched on the first part of empowerment in Chapter 2, where we saw how uncertainty was part of a recipe for making Terribleness the right approach to leadership. Logically, therefore, uncertainty and empowerment are directly in opposition, making it clear that we need to deal firmly with this first aspect of empowerment. This can be achieved through a number of techniques, and I would recommend that you use a selection of these rather than simply relying on one or two.

Try avoiding specific conversations about targets and goals. This simply paints too clear a framework for performance for your people. If you give people a target, they just seem to get good at hitting it, and this in turn can drive chirpiness and over-confidence — i.e. things you don't want. You will probably have to sit down with each of your employees once a year to conduct their appraisal and to talk about their goals for the next year, and quite right too, this is an excellent opportunity to diminish their sense of self-worth and extort a percentage of their bonus. But — don't fall into the trap of setting up parameters that are too easy to understand, otherwise your employees will have a tendency to run along, achieve things and then come back and start making your life difficult with an over-blown sense of their own efficacy. Instead, set targets that are, by definition, hard to hit and intangible. Here are some good ones I like to use:

- Create a culture of openness and collaboration in your team — ongoing.
- Improve reporting standards — end Q2.
- Have more impact — especially with senior people.
- Build the voice of the customer into the product development process.

These goals are, by definition, unachievable. Faced with this kind of objective, your people might come back and make a very good argument as to why they have achieved them, but you can simply state your expectations around what 'openness and collaboration' or 'improve' or 'more' actually means and give them the lowest rating possible. Most of us have an in-built tendency to set targets

> Set targets that are, by definition, hard to hit and intangible.

like this, and if you review your team's targets and find lots like these, then well done — you're on your way to breaking any sense of empowerment in your team. If, on the other hand, you find lots of laser-guided precision targets, use the following mnemonic to remember the Terrible approach to goal setting:

S = Subjective — allow plenty of room for 'discussion' and interpretation.

C = Contributes — i.e. anything they do focus on should contribute *directly* to your bonus.

A = Arguable — make sure there is plenty of wriggle room in case you need to wriggle later.

B = Broad — try to keep things high level.

Some Sissy leaders will talk about SMART objectives. Now you can knowingly say that you don't do SMART objectives (which are for Sissies — though perhaps don't say that out loud) because you have progressed to SCAB objectives, which are more advanced. Setting good SCAB objectives will keep your direct reports in a real muddle regarding accountability, but it isn't just in the objective setting that you can undermine empowerment.

To reduce clarity of accountability forming, you can also give lots of people similar work to do in an ill-defined way. This is an excellent approach due to a well-known trait of all human beings — territoriality. We are animals just like any other. Most animals mark their territory by urinating on the places where they go regularly, or rubbing a scent gland in the same way. (Incidentally, in some Terrible leadership trials we tried to imitate this behaviour, but found that urinating in your own or others' offices generally did little to increase perceived Terribleness. If you are keen to adopt this very animalistic behaviour we would definitely recommend limiting your urinatory excursions to other people's offices rather than your own. And for female Terrible leaders, use a She-wee, available online.) Like animals, we become defensive over our territory, but if we don't know precisely what our territory is, our first instinct is to fight the people around us to establish it. By setting overlapping objectives and accountabilities, you make sure that people expend most of their energy fighting each other rather than undermining you. This is a good way of giving people productive work to do without endangering your career. And if you doubt the fact that this *is* good productive work consider that, in the wild, young animals fight each other to prepare them for a future of fighting to survive. It is the same principle here — you are simply helping them sharpen their claws. The strongest will emerge, unscathed. The weaker ones will end up dishevelled, disheartened and disengaged. This is talent management in action. You reassign the weaker ones to other projects, and you keep a watchful eye on the successful ones — these are your competition...

Finally, try and be fairly fluid with regard to 'permission to proceed'. It is a good idea to intimate that you *have* granted permission for your direct reports to get on with their job. It helps, however, if you can occasionally, temporarily and without reason, suspend this. This keeps people on their toes and makes sure they don't take you for granted. If you notice a lapse in quality, it is a good idea to temporarily enforce a 'nothing moves unless I say so' policy for a couple of weeks, or until you get bored of it. Have everyone send all emails to you for checking before they can send them to anyone else. This will create a horrific log-jam on the one hand, but on the upside, it really undermines your people's sense of empowerment. And what do we **not** want? Em**power**ment!

So, in summary, to undermine any sense of emerging accountability, clarity and permission to proceed to the first facet of Empowerment (in turn the first of our 4Es) it helps if you can:

1. Set SCAB objectives.
2. Set overlapping objectives to encourage territorial behaviour.
3. Be fluid with permission.

But there is more to empowerment than accountability. Our second line of attack is around skills and competencies. People with clear accountability and permission to act but without the necessary skills and competencies are great fun to watch. Imagine a zoo that hires a new crocodile keeper and assigns them to the Head of the Reptile House. This head of section is only a beginner in the dark arts of Terrible Leadership and starts off on the wrong foot regarding empowerment. Instead of setting SCAB objectives they set SMART ones, making it painfully clear what the new crocodile keeper is expected to do:

Crocodile Keeper To-Do list:

1. Feed crocodiles by hand once a day so that crocodiles take food directly from the hand in front of paying public (they love to see this kind of thing).
2. Illustrate to aforementioned paying public that it is perfectly safe to sit on a crocodile provided you keep very still — once a day.
3. Brush crocodile's teeth by hand for three minutes twice a week.
4. Clean out crocodile pen every other day.

Our new recruit is thrilled with this level of clarity but they are inexperienced in handling four-metre crocodiles, a point which they are keen to make early on. Our head of section, having made a textbook error from the get go, recovers poise and Terribleness by explaining that the best place to learn is on the job and that they have every confidence in man's, not to mention crocodile's, capacity to learn. With this, they are packed off to the crocodile enclosure and left to get on with it. Place yourself now in the shoes of the new crocodile keeper. It should become obvious that accountability without the necessary skills and competencies required to complete the task you are accountable for tends to lead to a state of heightened anxiety. Which, of course, is excellent — the new recruit is likely to make mistake after mistake. Well, not in this scenario obviously, but in most normal office scenarios, mistakes tend to be less... terminal and therefore repeatable.

> Accountability without the necessary skills and competencies required to complete the task you are accountable for tends to lead to a state of heightened anxiety.

You can replicate these conditions for yourself by following a few simple rules:

- **Avoid developing people.** This means not just the obvious courses, coaching, training etc. It is easy to avoid these, just don't give people the time or opportunity to attend. However, watch out for the more insidious forms of learning, such as simple repetition. Limit this by moving people around so that they struggle to form a sense of mastery or capacity to complete a given task.

- **Avoid being clear about the skills and competencies necessary to do the job in the first place.** You need to be watchful if HR attempt to force you into writing a 'job description' or 'role profile'. This is a thinly-veiled plot to get you to write down all the accountabilities of and skills required by someone in a given role — something you would never normally do and something you should never be coerced into doing by HR. (If you're struggling to get HR off your back on this one, try reading Chapter 10 "Pushing HR over the edge").

- **Invent new competencies,** preferably ones that don't really exist, to keep people on their toes. Let's imagine that our crocodile keeper makes it through the first few months and comes to see the Head of Section. If they are now showing signs of real competence, it would be appropriate for the Head of Section to challenge them, wheel-chair-bound or otherwise, to get up to speed with how the digital world will impact crocodile keeping.
- **Keep some crocodiles in your office.** Again, check with local HR policy on this one, but if all else fails, they are a useful tool with which to make precisely this point.

You are now two-thirds of the way to totally eliminating empowerment in your team, and if you can remove two legs of a stool, you will find very few people able to sit on it. You might find one or two though who, through an unshakeable self-confidence, refuse to let go. For them, you have to take the issue head-on and deal with the root cause of their issue — their self-belief. Some people (self-deluded people), despite not knowing what it is they are supposed to do, nor having the necessary skills to do it, still seem to have a sense of self-belief and confidence that they can work it out, get good at it and succeed. (Now, if you're struggling with the logic required to not have the skills required to do something you are not clear about, then just ask yourself if your staff members have any significant skills at all? No — thought not, so let's remain confident on this point — they don't have the necessary skills for *whatever it is*).

These people still feel empowered, so your Terribleness has yet to be fully satisfied.

To get around this, you need to start chipping away at this sense of self-belief. You can do this in a number of ways, but open criticism is always a good place to start. Generally, as managers and leaders, we don't give anything like enough negative feedback. Every time our people do anything wrong, no matter how small, it is really important to point it out, make it seem more significant than it might really be, connect it with other similar mistakes they have made, even in the distant past, and throw in a few terms such as 'lazy' or 'stupid'. You can also demonstrate low confidence in their ability by asking to check everything they do. After a while, they will begin to share your low estimation of their competence and worth.

> After a while, they will begin to share your low estimation of their competence and worth.

So, there you go, a series of simple, practical steps (if you discount the idea about putting crocodiles in the office, this actually takes quite a lot of thought as it turns out they won't eat just 'anything') you can put in place to stifle, squash and totally eliminate any sense of burgeoning empowerment in your team. But, before you get all self-satisfied and bask in your new-found Terrible abilities, you are only one-quarter of your way through our Terrible 4Es. You still have Empathy, Engagement and Energy to deal with. There is work still to be done.

Empathy

Empathy is a more discrete idea than empowerment, and as such, it is a little easier to deal with. Empowerment is something your people will feel or not feel. Empathy is something you can demonstrate or not demonstrate, and as such, it is something intrinsically more in your power and control.

People who demonstrate high empathy make the worst Terrible leaders. Empathy involves placing yourself in the shoes of others; it means you are able to imagine and experience vividly the emotions and feelings of others. It typically results in responding to other people in such a way that shows real concern for their well-being and happiness. As you can imagine, this would undermine any attempt at retaining a Terrible leadership persona and brand and should be avoided at all costs. Many inexpert observers assume Terrible leaders take pleasure in the pain and discomfort of others. This is only partly true. Obviously, when the pain and discomfort of others is funny (like in most Japanese game shows), then yes, we take pleasure just like the next person. But when their pain and discomfort is embarrassing and awkward, we'd frankly rather not have anything to do with it. Like someone with facial warts.

No, the Terrible leader attempts to retain a state of unconsciousness regarding the emotional state of others. That allows us to act properly, Terribly and in the best interests of the organisation (well, ok, our bonus), not because we don't care about how people feel, but because we don't *know* how people feel. To avoid knowing, we must therefore avoid showing or having empathy with other people. We must remain very firmly in our own shoes, and keep out of the shoes of others. Just think: how much more happily would you borrow someone's jumper over someone's shoes? It's just not natural to stand in the shoes of others, so my advice is let the Sissies catch the verrucas and stick to your own footwear.

But to move away from shoe-driven analogy, here are some useful hints and tips to avoid the emotional turmoil brought on by too much empathy:

- **Don't ask too many questions.** You are paid to be an intuitive, switched-on leader. Trust your instincts and rely on them to tell you how your people are feeling — they probably couldn't articulate it very clearly even if you asked them.
- **Never paraphrase.** Sissy leaders do this to 'illustrate they have understood'. It is facile and makes you sound like a parrot. You're a leader. Not a parrot.
- **Prevent others from talking too much.** What you have to say is more important than what your people have to say, because you are the boss. This is logical. Therefore, it helps if you can prevent them from talking as much as you. You can normally achieve this by cutting across them mid-sentence. If this doesn't do the trick, just ask them politely, but firmly, to shut up because they are boring you.

To take these basic steps a little further, you can actually demonstrate a severe lack of empathy quite easily. This encourages your people to give up any shred of hope they may have entertained that you cared about them in any way, shape or form. Try deliberately getting the names of their partners wrong — do this persistently, even after having been corrected. For an even better impact, deliberately forget *their* name when you introduce them to clients or new members of staff — or use their predecessor's name. Repeatedly ask them to attend meetings when they have already told you they intend to be on holiday that week. If they're a vegetarian or Jewish, make a point of offering them a bacon sandwich. If they're a Muslim, make a point of always arranging to have your one-to-ones over an alcoholic beverage and act surprised when they order a Coke. If they've got a family, try and keep them hanging around for meetings when you know they are due to pick up their kids. All these tactics and many more can be used to drive home the fact that you are just not interested in your people as people, but instead as units of production.

Do we care how our cars are feeling? Of course not! Do we care if they're working? Hell yes! It's the same with your direct reports. Sissy leaders probably give their cars names, and they do the same with their people. Terrible leaders are more focused on results, and call their car 'the car' and their people, 'workers' or 'minions'. In this way, you can demonstrate the right level of empathy, which should prevent you from getting tangled up

> Do we care how our cars are feeling? Of course not! Do we care if they're working? Hell yes! It's the same with your direct reports.

in the issues and concerns of your people, while at the same time allowing you to drive their productivity and work rate with cheerfulness and cool detachment.

Right, so that's empowerment and empathy dealt with. We now have only to look at engagement and energy and you will be well on your way to keeping your people in a constant state of ineptitude, which, if you value your job, is exactly where you'll want them.

Engagement

Engagement is another one of these Sissy management mantras. Leadership consultants have made a lot of money blathering on about engagement this and engagement that. Essentially, they are talking about people having a meaningful connection with the work they do — i.e. they see it as more than 'just a job'. Which is ridiculous, because all your people do *is* 'just a job'. And a poor job of it they do too. Engaged people are passionate about their work. They think the work they do has real significance and value, both to the organisation and to the wider community.

On the plus side, from our perspective as Terrible leaders, engaged people tend to work harder and longer, by as much as 48% if research is to be believed. But, on the downside, engaged people are also likely to fight to see that the 'right' things are done as they see them, rather than blindly following your insightful directives. This is going to get trying after a while, and you need to take action now to prevent engagement from becoming a serious threat to your leadership.

Engagement stems partially from a clear line of sight between what an individual does and the results achieved by an organisation for their customers. Imagine a rope or a cord. An engaged person experiences pulling on the cord and seeing a direct, observable movement in something with intrinsic meaning and value to a customer (internal or external), i.e. their personal effort and observable results are directly connected. The best thing you can do is to cut this cord. The most direct, least subtle and most devastatingly effective approach is to give people work that is totally valueless and unconnected to anything a customer has ever wanted. Photocopying and most project planning fall into this category. Strategic reviews (which are ignored), communications plans, roadmaps and focus groups are also good things to keep people busy with and yet, at the same time, all will act to seriously diminish levels of engagement.

> Give people work that is totally valueless and unconnected to anything a customer has ever wanted. Photocopying and most project planning fall into this category.

When setting people off to do this kind of activity, it is best if you are vague with the instructions and desired outputs and woolly around due dates. Ask for results by the end of Q2, but if nothing appears until the end of the year, that's fine. That way, people get a clearer idea of the fact that the work they do is of no real significance or importance. Now, logically, you might think,

"How is this going to help me?" Still thinking like a bit of a Sissy, aren't we? Giving people monotonous, valueless, pointless things to do serves three fundamental purposes:

1. It prevents them from getting all engaged and cocky and threatening you in your job (which would be reason enough — but there are other huge benefits).

2. It builds the size of your team. We all know that the more people you have reporting to you, the more important you are and, therefore, the more money you will earn and the more good sex you will have. This is just the law. Now, finding meaningful, productive, focused work for lots of people to do is difficult and rather bottlenecks the pace at which you can bring people on board. Terrible leaders are not hampered by this concern. Instead, they scoop up as many people as possible, give them meaningless work to do (but lots of it) and watch the promotions roll in.

3. By now, you will be sold on the logical, sensible merits of this course of action — but wait, there's more. Because you can fill your people's working day in such a way that will have them questioning their self-worth and very existence on this planet, they do not have to be especially capable. Anyone can wallow in self-doubt and uncertainty. Even a complete dolt can become suicidally depressed as a result of a prolonged exposure to pointlessness and futility. You will never fail as a recruiting manager. You will be known far and wide as a manager who gets the most from their people. And you won't have to spend lots of time

sifting through CVs, you can just pick all the people with the most attractive photos and go with that. Simple. Once again, we see that Terrible leadership not only gets results, but it can also be simple, straightforward and fast.

There are other ways of disconnecting people's efforts from the delivery of value.

Rather than cutting the cord, you can just conceal what the cord is connected to. Imagine the cord leading into a cloud or a bank of fog. Your job now is to manage that cloud. A good way to make the connection unclear and uncertain is through complexity of organisational structures. If one person's effort links to another person's which, in turn, connects to another person and so on and so on until eventually it actually reaches someone who gives a damn (usually a customer), then only one person experiences the satisfaction of delivering to the person who cares. Everyone else is protected from the engagement this experience might foster. If people in the final customer-facing layer get a bit too good at their job, a bit too successful and a bit over-chirpy as a result there is a simple remedy. Just promote them to a role in one of the more removed layers, they'll soon lose their edge, quieten down and realise that the paycheck is more important than the end result.

Another way to make things cloudy and confused is to have lots of meetings (as much as 80–90% of your people's time should be engaged in meetings). This prevents people from doing anything of any value and gets them increasingly confused about what they are supposed to do and how it connects to what everyone else seems to be doing.

Cutting the cord between effort and real results, or at least concealing the connection in a thick fog of over-complexity, is a good start for reducing levels of engagement. But there is more you can do. Engaged people typically feel a connection to and sense of duty towards customers or clients. You can undermine this by pointing out the obvious, i.e. that the customer is a grasping, money-grubbing ne'er-do-well who would sooner spit at your mother than show a shred of loyalty or gratitude. If your people seem not to believe you on this point, this is very easily remedied by simply introducing them to a couple of customers periodically. Just ask them to come in, sit them in a room with your people under the guise of 'getting to know our customers' and then ask them, "What would you change about our service?". This works just as well with internal clients as it does with external ones. They will then proceed to list a string of impossible, unreasonable and fantastical desires. Thank them for their time, ask them to leave and then spend some time with your team laughing at their naivety and ridiculousness. Your team members may be a little hurt to discover that what you have said is true all along, that the customers are, in fact, stupid and unrealistic. You can demonstrate your empathy for this discomfort by telling them to grow up and act like adults. In this way you are practising Terrible engagement and Terrible empathy all in one go.

You are almost at the end of the 4Es, there is just the need to crack down on Energy and you will be there. But before we look at energy, let's just look at an interesting shared characteristic of empowerment, empathy and engagement. Quite often, you will find that your organisation, probably influenced by some Sissy in HR, has an annual survey that actually measures the levels of these three in your organisation. If you are lucky, they will play straight into your hands by actually giving you personalised results for your own team. This is excellent news, as it will give you an opportunity to check that levels are sufficiently low to avoid the likelihood of an impending coup. Good scores are around 25% positive response and lower. Ideally, you want less than a quarter of all people feeling empowered, empathised with and engaged. In a perfect world, it would be 0%, but this is unlikely to ever be fully realised (unless you can set up a police state, but then the police typically get quite engaged, you can see the problem...). Aim for 25% and then try and bring that number down little by little, year after year, using the techniques described above. The old adage is absolutely true: if you can measure it, you can manage it. You may get someone from HR poking their nose in to try and understand or even raise your scores. Sissies think these scores should be high, and rather than try and correct them on this obvious error, there is a foolproof way of putting them off the scent. Simply make sure you do a reorganisation of your staff every year and blame the low scores on that. HR always nod wisely on receiving this explanation and will see this as reasonable. They change the HR person every 12 months or so anyway, because they are probably useless and ineffective, so when you use the same excuse next year, they'll still believe you. An annual reorganisation is a good idea anyway for a number of reasons:

- It creates a heightened sense of uncertainty and anxiety, especially if you put people at the risk of redundancy. Generally though, it is a bad idea to let anyone actually leave the organisation as they are serving a valuable purpose by inflating your staff numbers and therefore justifying your salary. At the last minute, find them a new project role to do, ideally something that is fairly meaningless and vacuous (see points on engagement above). They will then feel relieved and lucky to still be around, which is exactly where you want them — low-confidence pawns to use and abuse at your discretion.

- It provides an additional annual project which you will need to recruit people to run. If you can stretch this out, you can justify keeping these people on full-time to reorganise your department. Aim to have around 5–10% of your staff employed looking at how best to configure the department at all times.

If HR don't play into your hands and run the survey for you, it is a good idea to do one yourself. True Terrible leaders are sticklers for professionalism, so just because HR aren't measuring the 4Es, doesn't mean to say you shouldn't be. The questionnaire approach is good because it will allow people to answer honestly. If you ask people directly if they are engaged in their work and feel empowered, they, being afraid that the wrong answer could lead to the sack, will answer in the way they believe you want them to, i.e. they will say yes. This will defeat the object and your scores will be really high. You could feed these results to HR if you want (it might help you get promoted), but you also need to check that the real underlying scores are as low as they should be.

If you can't face the thought of writing and sending out a questionnaire, you could ask a Sissy leader from another department to come and ask a few questions, with the clear agreement that all data will remain anonymous (obviously you don't *really* mean that, but it helps if you say it). Speaking to this Sissy, your people are more likely to spill the beans about their real experience of your leadership. Ask the Sissy to come to your office to share the results and specifically ask that they do not share them with anyone else before they share them with you. When they bring you their report, it should reflect a dispirited, cowed, disengaged, unempowered, uncared-for staff. The more shocked and appalled the Sissy leader is, the better you have done your job. Unlike them, your people pose no threat to your leadership and you shall remain in the post until you are able to move up. Now, obviously, this Sissy leader is in possession of some very dangerous information. Ask to take all their notes, original and typed up, to allow you to 'review them overnight' and promise you'll talk to HR in the morning. Then have them followed and killed. Then burn all the papers and their

> The more shocked and appalled the Sissy leader is, the better you have done your job.

computer, if you can get hold of it. In some countries, it is quite expensive to have people killed, and in those same countries, it is often also difficult to pass this off as a legitimate business expense. Think about conducting the process every other year if annual silencing contracts prove un-economical.

Energy

Moving now to the last of our 4Es — Energy. It should be obvious by now that people with too much energy are incredibly dangerous. They are the ones most likely to spot your deliberate plots to disempower and disengage. You need to try and maintain a background level of entropy and apathy.

One way to do this can be learned by carefully observing parties. If we throw a party at our house, we want it to be like the ones out of *Breakfast at Tiffany's*, with seemingly endless friends and acquaintances crammed into every conceivable nook and cranny. All the best parties happen in the kitchen and the stairs, but only when there are also lots of people filling up the living room, dining room, garden and bedrooms.

> It should be obvious by now that people with too much energy are incredibly dangerous.

In the same way, energy in organisations is considerably higher in buzzy, full offices. You can prevent this from happening by working with your facilities team to keep people spread apart. Keep to a policy of very low worker densities in your office, and make sure people can't see each other over tall dividers, or better yet, cubicles. This prevents people from talking, getting to know one another, making friends or becoming energised.

You can take other measures to reduce the level of simmering, insurrection fuelling energy in your team. Here are some quick hints and tips:

- Have the air-conditioning system adjusted to deliver slightly lower levels of oxygen to keep people sleepy.
- Aim to house staff in large square buildings. This keeps natural light down to a minimum.
- Replace any windows that can be opened with ones that are permanently sealed shut — in order to prevent ventilation and the entry of fresh air.
- Make coffee and tea freely available, but make people pay for fresh water. Put bottles in a vending machine and have no taps apart from the ones in the toilet — people don't like to drink from those. Too much caffeine (more than three or four cups in a day) rather than waking us up actually dulls our senses and makes us irritable and crabby.
- Make sure the food served in the canteen is heavy, carbohydrate-based food. Fries, burgers, potatoes, pasta, fried battered fish, curry, sugary deserts and cakes are all good. These foods give people a quick boost, but will leave people feeling sloth-like and useless for most of the day. Avoid salads, nuts, fruits, fish, porridge etc. These foods not only release energy evenly over many hours but they also make people feel virtuous and smug, which is an unpleasant side effect.
- If there is a gym in the office, close it.

- Discourage people from cycling to work by removing showers and changing facilities. This is valuable space and can be used to decrease the seating density of your staff (i.e. give them more room) so that energy dissipates more effectively.

If you are successful, you should be able to convert your staff into a dull-witted, dispirited dejected bunch of no-hopers who are totally reliant on you and your superior qualities.

Once again, it is in these little details that true Terribleness can be exercised and perfected. It is very unlikely that anyone else will notice your efforts, no one will thank you and no one will have an inkling that you are trying to stifle people's treacherous energies. The Terrible leader is at once bold and overt yet subtle and covert. By managing the 4Es of empowerment, empathy, engagement and energy, you will ensure that while your Sissy colleagues are deposed, sidelined and rejected, your star will continue to shine, untarnished and unmolested by your grasping, cringing direct reports. If you are successful, you should be able to convert your staff into a dull-witted, dispirited dejected bunch of no-hopers who are totally reliant on you and your superior qualities. This state of affairs leaves you with a challenge and an opportunity.

Challenge

Having created these conditions, how do you ensure that a sufficient level of productive work is achieved at all? In the next chapter (8), we will look at how you can use some Terrible techniques to motivate your people to deliver a sufficient level of work so that your team, department or organisation are sufficiently profitable, productive and well-perceived to guarantee your own ongoing successful career.

Opportunity

Having created these conditions, you now have a series of fantastic opportunities. In Chapter 9, we will look at how you can enjoy the vacuum of self-direction, optimism and energy that you have created. True Terrible leaders don't just create the conditions for Terribleness, they take advantage of them. What's the point of being Terrible if you can't enjoy it a little...

Chapter Seven — Lessons in Terrible

- Your useless minions, despite looking harmless and ugly are in fact your greatest threat and need to be managed as such.
- You need to reduce the 4Es (Empowerment, Empathy, Engagement and Energy) to the lowest possible levels:
  - Reduce empowerment by eliminating all clarity around objectives by following SCAB methodology.
  - Prevent people from developing any skills of capabilities by preventing them from attending training and by moving them around a lot.
  - Erode self-belief by being relentlessly critical.
  - Practice low empathy in order to avoid finding out how people are feeling: never ask questions and ask people to shut up.
  - Prevent a sense of engagement emerging by disconnecting people's efforts from meaningful results.
  - Help your staff see the customer (internal or external) for the naive, unrealistic, selfish people they really are.
  - Reduce energy by keeping people spread out in the office, closing the gym and discouraging people from cycling to work.

Chapter Seven — Lessons in Terrible

- Use HR-administered surveys to check the level of engagement or empowerment is low. If there is no staff survey in your organisation, ask a Sissy leader to conduct some research on your behalf (but silence them lest they blab to your boss).
- Read Chapter 8 in order to balance a low 4E score with plenty of output and productivity.
- Read Chapter 9 in order to take full advantage of your wonderfully low 4E scores.

Terrible leaders are wise to the threat posed by their staff. Rather than bury their head in the sand, they take carefully calculated measures to keep their team members miserable and dispirited at all times. Can you afford to take any other course of action?

CHAPTER 8
MOTIVATION FOR TERRIBLE LEADERS

In the previous chapter on 'Making them Miserable', we focused on creating the right conditions within your team to ensure that your own leadership position is never threatened. This is, if you like, a logical first step on your way to becoming a true Terrible leader. It is a necessary foundation of Terribleness, you can get everything else wrong but if you have kept empowerment, empathy, engagement and energy at the lowest possible levels, you will still go far. However, there is more to the fully-fledged, fully-rounded Terrible leader than just squashing the spirit of your direct reports. Terrible leaders are achievers. Under their reign much is done, and typically it is done fast.

Hitler is a good example. Again, it is not for me to question his philosophy, approach or actions (my great grandmother was a German Jew before anyone writes any letters about this next bit), but his achievements and his pace were undeniably staggering. Most of us in his position would have annexed Austria and then had a biscuit. Not Hitler. He really went for it, and in a few short years, had declared war on just about the whole known world. Now, arguably, here he over-extended himself, something a true Terrible leader would be careful to avoid. Hitler was not the most subtle. But whatever his shortcomings, his example serves to remind us that the truly Terrible not only keep competitors at bay, they also keep those would-be-competitors in a heightened state of productivity. Partly, they achieve this by setting up cleverly overlapping objectives, as was discussed in the previous chapter (Goering, Hess, Heydrich and Goebbels seem to have spent most of the Nazi regime in-fighting), but Terrible leaders also carefully manage the incentive structure of their minions.

In this chapter, we will explore the Terrible approach to incentives and motivation and what you can do to ensure that your people, despite being up to their necks in a slough of despond, are still doing everything they can to ensure the future success of your career. The American political and military machine understood the subtle balance of incentive and motivation as they invaded Iraq the second time round in 2003. I'm not totally sure who said this, but they were important and it amounted to the US Carrot and Stick approach to Iraq:

> **Stick** = *Think* of not co-operating and we'll park enough ordnance up your fundament to ensure future generations of Iraqis shit metal until judgement day.
>
> **Carrot** = co-operate and we won't use the stick.

It's the subtlety that stands out here. By attending to both the repercussions of negative behaviour and the benefits of positive behaviour, the Americans had on the table a deal the Iraqis just couldn't refuse. And they didn't. Sissy management books will probably talk in detail about the nature of PUSH and PULL when it comes to motivation and influence. By the way, motivation, influence, manipulation, coercion — these are all words that mean the same thing, namely, '*ways of making you do things you didn't initially want to do*'. We try and talk in terms of motivation and influence (we mean manipulation and coercion really), largely to keep HR off our backs and also to reduce the chances of us slipping up and accidentally asking our minions how manipulated they are feeling instead of how motivated they are feeling. It comes to the same thing.

BUT, back to the Sissy management books and their PUSH and PULL factors. The idea here is that 'push' factors are things that drive behaviour by making the repercussions of not doing something more unpleasant or more unfavourable than the thought of doing the thing itself. We can illustrate this with a little example. Ask yourself, do you want to eat a live frog? Of course not. There is insufficient 'push' in the mix. Let's try this instead: I have kidnapped all of your friends and family, everyone you have ever cared for. I have assigned each of them to a highly-skilled torturer who has the clamps, picks and scalpels warmed up and ready to go for a proper three-day session. I'll let them go unharmed if you eat a live frog. Yum! You'd eat a plateful, wouldn't you? This is how 'push' works.

The alternative to 'push' is 'pull'. Pull factors drive behaviour by making the potential reward for doing something so pleasant and alluring that it more than offsets the unpleasantness of having to do the something in the first place. So, put that live frog back on your plate — still doesn't look appetising, does it? Now, let's say I'll give you a million dollars if you eat it. Frog? What frog? I'm not sure you even chewed that one! Couldn't get it down fast enough, eh? Just in case I change my mind — very sensible. Here's your million bucks. This is how push and pull works, and it is the same principle as carrot and stick. However, what Sissy management books fail to point out are two fundamental truths about the manipulation of your fellow human beings that you *have* to understand in order to make it as a Terrible leader:

1. The best carrots are the absence of the best sticks (see US/ Iraq example above). If you get the right stick, all you need to do is not use it and you've also got a fantastic carrot.

2. Push and pull are not equally effective. If you've got to get people to do things, push wins over pull every time.

> If you've got to get people to do things, push wins over pull every time.

We'll take each of these fundamental truths in turn and explore what they mean for us as Terrible leaders. First, let's get the right stick...

The problem with people is that they are all different. In an ideal world, and perhaps in a future world, all minions will conform to strict specifications. Until then you are going to have to get it into your head that the most effective sticks are different for different people. If you think about this, it makes sense. Some of us are afraid of scorpions, others keep them as pets. I'm terrified of expensive handbags, whereas my wife seems to really like them and is comfortable with several in the house, whereas just the *thought* of one gives me sleepless nights. Different strokes for different folks, as the saying goes. As Terrible leaders, we could perhaps borrow this sentiment, '*different sticks for different ...*' (you can fill in the rest).

The most effective sticks are the most extreme ones. Pain, suffering, hunger and Big Brother typically generate the most extreme responses. These are difficult to use within a modern office environment however (although kudos to you if you do manage it — award yourself some Terrible bonus points), so it pays to think a little more creatively about the sticks we can use in a typical working day. One trick with sticks (and with incentives in general) is to identify an intrinsic aspect of a person's daily working life that they like and threaten to take it away from them unless they do as they're told. To make life a little bit easier for us, people do generally fall into three broad categories.

Category One

People who are intrinsically motivated by hitting targets or getting things done — theorists (McClelland etc.) call this the need for achievement; we'll call them the *workers*. The best sticks for this kind of person are anything that takes away their ability to rate and understand their own personal performance. What we learned in the previous chapter about SCAB objectives will be particularly effective for this group of people in terms of keeping their levels of engagement and empowerment at record low levels. But to get them moving and working towards your next promotion here are some great sticks to use:

1. Threaten to scrap all team or individual targets (such as you have allowed to exist in the first place) and instead everyone will be asked to work together unless performance improves. (This will actually appeal to Category two people — see below — so this is quite a targeted approach.)

2. If they are working on something that's quite hard to do and you want to get them working harder on it, simply suggest that perhaps this job is a little tough for them and perhaps they'd like it if they could do an easy job for a little while. Workers love challenge and hate easy jobs, just watch performance levels rocket...

3. If you want to see more output from them, threaten to get some of the department's dead beat employees to come and help them for a couple of months. Workers don't like dead weight, they hate anything that dilutes their own sense of achievement, so carrying a couple of losers won't appeal, instead they'll redouble their efforts.

4. If they look like they're not going to hit the necessary figures, threaten to change the goalposts. e.g. if they're supposed to bring in new accounts, threaten to change their goal to a customer satisfaction focus at the end of quarter two. They'll hate that. Give them the option of keeping the old target with a slight increase in output and they'll take it and burn some midnight oil.

5. When they join the team, make it clear to them that you expect them to be promoted within two years. They'll aim for that like a Cruise Missile. At around 18 months, begin the process of moving that promotion further away unless performance output increases. You can keep this up for years. They'll flog themselves silly for as long as it takes for them to get the hint that they'll never get promoted, then they'll leave, but in the meantime – wow, they'll get *loads* done.

The workers are probably the most important group of people for you as a Terrible leader. They generally just like getting on with things (they're not always the brightest) and many seem to believe that people will judge them and promote them on the basis of their hard work. Of course, we know that's not true and that, in reality, you get promoted based on your Terribleness, but it's useful to have lots of these workers around. They are the most straightforward, malleable and generally the easiest to

> Many seem to believe that people will judge them and promote them on the basis of their hard work. Of course, we know that's not true.

abuse of all the groups. Just give them lots to do, stand back and watch them get on with it. It helps if you can create plenty of competition between individuals and teams, as workers will enjoy the sense of winning and work extra hard to avoid the feeling of losing. Most industries attract workers, and it is likely that anything between 30% and 60% of your workforce is comprised of workers, which is good news for the Terrible ones amongst us...

Category Two

People who are intrinsically motivated by having meaningful relationships with others, who like to belong to a group and worry less about what they are doing and more about who they are doing it with; we'll call this group of people *softies*.

Despite being mentally subnormal (obviously) and wrong in the head, these people actually respond marvellously well to correctly constructed sticks. But be careful! Many of the sticks for workers actually work as bonafide carrots for softies. They don't like specific individual targets much and would far rather work in an ambiguous, collective style where everyone has to work together. If you offer them the department's biggest losers to work with, they'll probably misinterpret this as an indication of your trust in their ability to develop even the completely useless. So, be careful not to use the same stick on a softie as you'd use with a worker. But some great sticks for softies include:

1. Explain that unless productivity increases, you are going to have to make some redundancies. Now, you need to be careful here. If you make it sound like the softie themselves is at threat of redundancy, they will enter into a state of blind panic and withdraw into their shell completely. Instead, drop some not so subtle hints about who would be let go first. For maximum effect, pick out the weakest, most vulnerable people in the team.

Someone who's just been diagnosed with something nasty and life-threatening, the new parent struggling to pay a mortgage, the young person in their first job. Obviously, you don't intend to actually make these people redundant, but the intimation will drive your softie to whole new levels of productivity.

2. Explain that unless work rates increase, you are going to need to move people further apart to allow them to focus on their work. Softies love to chat, and they think that it is their right to chat away for as much as 80% of the day. Show them a small desk in a remote corner far from anyone or anything and tell them you've been thinking about locating them there. They'll crawl over broken glass to avoid the lonely corner!

3. Softies hate competition. Instead, they love collaboration and togetherness and fluffy bunnies and marshmallows and baby deer. So, to get them to up the work rate, tell them that unless you see a marked improvement, you are going to introduce a monthly meeting where each team leader needs to argue for and justify continued investment in their team or project. If that fails, bring in some baby deer and threaten to have them shot in the car park at lunch time unless everyone gets cracking.

Softies are very common, but they are not evenly distributed across industries. If you work in high finance, investment banking, oil exploration or the gambling industry, you are probably not going to have that many in your team. However, if you work in the public sector, it is likely that as much as 40–50% of your minions are softies. This might seem alarming, but don't worry — as a Terrible leader you work with what you've got and, with the right stick, even a softie can be induced to significant levels of performance.

The other good thing about softies is that they are loyal, even to Terrible leaders. This may seem strange, but softies suffer from a condition we might technically call 'inter-group bias'. This means they attach a disproportionate amount of significance and importance to belonging to a given group. A lot of their individual identity gets caught up in their group affiliation. You've all met them at dinner parties. These are the people who seem to think it is interesting and significant that they work for some unknown person in some unheard-of department in some obscure organisation. No one else cares, but they seem fascinated by it. This is because they do not have the strongest sense of individuality and instead borrow information about who they are and what they do from the groups to which they belong. This means a couple of things for the Terrible leader.

Firstly, you can push these people a long way before they'll crack. Workers are more cynical, if they sense you're kicking them mercilessly they'll put up with it for as long as you can credibly hold out the fake carrot of promotion. Softies, being less results orientated, worry less about promotion, but instead worry endlessly about losing membership of the group from which they leech a sense of meaning and identity, i.e. they fear redundancy more than they seek promotion. Secondly, you can trust these people to represent your department in inter-departmental meetings. Workers will just go along and work out logically whether departments should collaborate or not. This could be disastrous. Softies, on the other hand, will be all warm and fluffy to begin with, but because they have such a strong sense of belonging to their own group, they will see all other groups as suspicious and inferior.

Category Three

People who are motivated by power, a sense of control and influence. We will call these people the *slicks*. Slicks are by far the most dangerous category of employees. It is from this category that most Terrible leaders will emerge. They are less interested in clear targets and working with other people, but instead more interested in working with senior people and on high-profile projects. They are interested in having their opinion listened to and generally think they know best about nearly everything. They won't do anything unless they can see how it contributes to their future success and they hate 'busy work'.

All of this means that it is the slicks who represent your clearest threat (they are most like you) and, at the same time, should be easiest to keep at a good level of productivity because, if nothing else, you should have an insight into their scheming, Machiavellian mind. Here's some tips to get you started:

1. Explain that there are two important pieces of work to achieve in the next quarter. One involves working on a

project to be presented to the CEO or some other grand poobah, while the other involves working on a project that will be presented to a bunch of homeless flunkies. If they don't sharpen up their act, they'll be on flunky duty.

2. Set them up as advisors to some strategic committee or other (there are always loads of these) and every time you need them to exert a little more effort, suggest that perhaps their advisory role needs to be reviewed in order to allow them to focus on the 'day job'. They'll move heaven and earth to stay on as special advisors.

3. When they start giving their opinion or their ideas in meetings suggest that perhaps when they can be relied upon to deliver against their existing objectives they will then be permitted to share their views on everything else, but until then they'd best focus on doing their own jobs. This will fire them up to achieve more in their role.

Slicks are the least common type of people. You may have as little as 5–10% in your teams, although this rises to 30–40% in management layers and in more entrepreneurial industries. They are a tricky and petulant group to lead and manage and do tend to get stroppy and sulk if they don't get their way. They are much harder to pin down than workers or softies, who generally behave more or less as sheep and can be herded easily enough with a strong hand.

To keep slicks performing, it is important to create an environment where they have a lot of privileges which you can then remove one at a time in order to keep them feeling sufficiently motivated to perform. This requires a little bit more in terms of careful planning and forethought than the other groups, but you will find it well worth it in the long term as you keep your slicks running hard to cling onto their status as special this or special that.

A good trick to bear in mind for slicks is their total susceptibility to hierarchy and titles. They are complete suckers for incremental and meaningless changes in their job titles for example. If today they are an executive administrative assistant you will find they will break their balls to be made a senior executive administrative assistant. They will miss the fact that their role doesn't change at all as a result of this momentous promotion, and you won't even need to stretch the budget, as they are normally happy with the new title alone.

In the US, many organisations have developed a whole series of excellent mechanisms to keep slicks happy (we have been slow to adopt or too quick to throw out these ideas in Europe). Many companies have strict

> They are complete suckers for incremental and meaningless changes in their job titles.

allowances on things like office or cubicle carpet depth, calendar size and pot plant height depending on your relative seniority. Pot plants are a great example. You can promote a slick to an infinitesimally more senior role and illustrate this with a pot plant that is 5cm taller. They'll love this! It seems incredible, but it's true, and more to the point, they'll work their butts off for you to secure the new title on their email and the slightly taller plant. And how much does this cost you? Exactly — nothing...

People often ask me how you can tell which category a given minion is in. This is difficult, and the best bet is to threaten them with each stick in turn and see which one gets them performing to the highest level. Alternatively, try these observation notes to try and work out who is who:

Workers
- Will probably talk about how much they have achieved, how fast or how many.
- Will send brief emails which are very to the point.
- Will not be very interested in the private lives of others.
- Will be quite competitive at office away days (if you have any).

Softies
- Will have a box of tissues on their desk.
- May cry from time to time (inexplicably).
- Will speak softly and in a roundabout way.
- Will send long emails with lots of exclamation marks.
- Will be very interested in the private lives of others.
- Will have a cat.

Slicks
- Will suck up to senior people.
- Will ignore mundane work that doesn't get seen by more senior people.

- Will get sulky if their opinions aren't listened to.
- Will talk lots about senior people.
- Will be interested in and talk about promotion a lot.

This is the science of Terrible leadership, it requires experimentation and careful observation. If you're still not quite sure try the *worker* sticks to begin with, as workers typically constitute the highest number of employees, then work through *softie* and finally the *slick* sticks. You'll soon see which threats have your employees spinning in their executive chairs. In all of these cases, you are creating carrots (or 'pull' factors) through the absence of the sticks you are threatening to use.

Sissy management handbooks will give you a lot of guff about the need to find things to motivate your people, whereas we know as Terrible leaders that the best carrots are the absence of the best sticks. Simply by offering not to hit someone with a well-crafted, psychologically targeted stick, you are creating exactly the conditions you need for frenetic activity.

> The best carrots are the absence of the best sticks.

As JFK said, "*Ask not what you can give your employees to motivate them, but what you can threaten to take away that would really upset them*". That might not be the precise quote, but it was something along these lines. This completes 'Terrible Lesson One' with respect to motivation: the best carrots are the absence of the best sticks. Now it is time to turn our attention to 'Terrible Lesson Two'...

When you were a small child, say around seven or eight, your parents, grandparents, or nanny or that wolf that looked after you in the jungle, whatever it was that brought you up, they probably read you some stories. Think back on those stories. They were simple, formulaic tales of heroes and derring do. They probably all had something in common and ran along the following lines...

Plot for identikit fairy tale

Once upon a time, there was a beautiful princess. She was young, slender, attractive, and crucially, she was not a slapper (she had err... kept herself to herself, if you get my meaning). She was nice to animals and didn't get drunk at the weekends. She was afflicted with one or more of the following ailments: evil stepmother, evil stepsisters, a curse that turned her into an ugly crone at night, frizzy hair, or general monsterism. In any case, one or more of these unfortunate ailments ended up placing her in a remote castle with barely adequate toilet facilities. It is unclear what the catering provision at the castle is, but it is plausible that forest animals bring berries.

The castle is guarded by a fearsome, fire-breathing dragon called Dargon or Gordan or Nodgar. Probably not Nodgar on reflection, but the dragon's name is never Simon or Champ. The princess is in a tricky predicament, but fortunately, her elderly father, or a passing hermit or a forest animal (bird, squirrel, crab etc.) gets to hear of her inauspicious housing arrangements and gets the word out to the local princes. The word on the street is that whoever can rescue said princess from said evil-named dragon is allowed to sleep with her and inherit her father's kingdom. For the sake of the children, the 'sleeping with' part is normally glossed over and instead 'marriage' is discussed, but we all know what's really going on. Essentially, the elderly king is pimping out his daughter in order to get rid of a dragon. It seems cold, but we've all been there.

Princes come forward in an alarmingly unsuitable array of heavy armour and are variously broiled, chewed and torn limb from limb by Nodgar the dragon. Finally, some young man whose parentage is unclear and who is currently engaged in cleaning out the royal stables, or some other honourable and manual occupation, comes forward and sets out on his own armed only with a broom and last week's edition of 'Top Joust'. He slays the dragon using a well-balanced combination of wit, strength and bravery *or* discovers the dragon is only cranky because no one calls him by his proper name, which is Simon. The Princess falls head over heels in love, the boy turns out to be some long-lost prince anyway and everyone lives happily ever after.

This is a formula we are all well acquainted with and it serves as a metaphor for much of the rest of our lives. People do things for one of two reasons, both of which are illustrated in our identikit fairytale. The first reason is to avoid something bad, i.e. getting eaten by a dragon. Much of the actual activity undertaken by our valiant princes (successful or broiled) involves lances, swords, running around and last minute swerves. All of this activity is generated by the presence of the dragon. If you remove the princess, they would still need to do all of this to avoid getting eaten alive. The second reason for doing something is to get something good, i.e. sleeping with, sorry, 'marrying' the princess (remember she is a hottie, if she were ugly this whole thing falls down a bit). A small portion of the activity undertaken by our princes is down to the princess alone; setting out in the first place, packing some snacks, feeding the horse, combing their hair etc. The crucial and Terrible truth here is that more of what the princes actually do is dragon-related than it is princess-related. And this is true in everyday life too...

> More of what the princes actually do is dragon-related than it is princess-related.

At the beginning of this chapter, I said that if you really need to get people to do things, stick wins over carrot every time. From our fairytale, we might re-term this, *"If you need to get people to do things, dragons win over princesses every time"*. Even Barack Obama knew this when he was campaigning against John McCain for the US presidency in 2009. The princess in that situation was himself, the thought of an articulate, left of centre, black, intelligent man who was not George Bush. But Obama knew this alone would not be enough and he focused his campaign on what would happen if people did not vote for him: the dragon. As humans, we respond to dragons far more than we respond to princesses. We move away from unpleasantness more willingly and more immediately than we move towards good things. This is something Sissy management books won't tell you. The challenge for us Terrible leaders is to arm ourselves with a powerful set of dragons that can motivate even the most lacklustre employee.

> We move away from unpleasantness more willingly and more immediately than we move towards good things.

Think about it: in wartime, countries get ever so organised and everyone pulls together. There is a clearly defined enemy that everyone understands and fears. Collective action is made much easier and action unthinkable in peacetime becomes possible. Necessity is the mother of invention, as the saying goes. It is the same with motivating your employees. Notice that in our story, the princes generally disappear into the forest one at a time to get variously disposed of until our hero enters the scene. In real organisational life, you will need your people to complete complex tasks together. This means you have to find a universally attractive princess (very hard to do, for example, what if some of the princes were gay, that never seems to get a mention...) that everyone agrees is worth getting organised in order to save. Sissy management books call this a '*vision of the future*' or some other vacuous statement. They would argue that if everyone is clear about this wonderful attractive vision and what it means for them, they will all, in unison, head off into the forest and look for the princess. This is tosh. They will all bugger about in different bits of the forest, build camps, fight each other, get lost, find a goat and mistake *it* for the princess. This is the Sissy way, the Terrible way is not to explain the princess to your people. The princess is your own personal prize: power, money and promotion. Why would you want anyone sharing your personal princess? Exactly. So keep her hidden away and deal strictly in dragons.

With a clear, well-articulated dragon, you don't trust your employees to go out proactively into a strange forest; instead, you bring the dragon to them and let them deal with it. If they don't deal with it, they will get eaten (or have their careers destroyed), and this is no bad thing. Business is about dealing with dragons, so if you can't manage, then it's probably best you stood aside and let the professional dragon wranglers have a go. Just have a think about your direct reports. Picture them in your mind's eye. Would you trust them to head off together into the woods and look for princesses? I didn't think so. No, you are far better off dealing in scaly monsters.

So, now let's move on to how...

The first, most important and most instantly accessible dragon is you. You can breathe fire (shout). You can fly (be more senior). You can bite (sack them or bother them in some other way). You must ask yourself, "How scary is my dragon?". If your dragon is a smoky, stunted, slightly ill-looking reptilian thing, no one is going to run around at the right level of panic in order to get anything done. All you will achieve is being avoided. No, your dragon must be a towering inferno of rage and destructive power. When you rear up to your full height, you must block out all the light and leave people trembling and weak at the knees. Your name must be dread. You must be Terrible indeed to behold. Let's look at some handy hints and tips.

1. **Volume:** you need to be aiming for around 110 decibels here, or about the same as a jumbo jet taking off. Things sound better when they're louder — and so do you. Practice by shouting outdoors with someone recording how loud you are and see how loud you can get. Try and shout at people from your stomach, not the back of your throat. Stand up straight, take big breaths and tilt your head forward like an opera singer. Try variations in the depth of your voice. Some people get more purchase if they talk in a high pitch, but most of you will find your voice becomes more Terrible if you drop it down a bit. Margaret Thatcher knew this and it got her elected as UK Prime Minister and there followed a reign of some considerable Terribleness.

    > Things sound better when they're louder — and so do you.

2. **Variation:** don't just shout. Sometimes, you will find you can be most withering by saying something very quietly and very slowly. Imagine you've messed up and you need to go and see your boss. All they do is look you in the eye and very quietly and very slowly say, "Get... out... of... my... sight...". This has real impact.

3. **Swear:** and I don't just mean in the obvious ways. F-words and C-words are all very well and should be used liberally to illustrate your ire but try and be a bit more creative. Threaten your employees that if they don't get a move

on, you will snap off their arms and then use the bleeding appendages to beat them to death. This sort of colourful phrase is more memorable and more motivating than simply shouting, "just f***ing do something".

4. **Get in people's faces:** dragons are more scary close up, so make sure that when you are shouting your curse-laden tirade, you do it a couple of centimetres away from your employees' faces.

5. **Get physical:** now — be careful here. Actually hitting, punching, biting or killing people, especially women, whilst a natural part of Terrible leadership in the good old days, gives your HR team a very easy target to aim for. Only hit people if you can be sure no one else will ever find out. If you *can* be sure no one will ever find out then aim for the nose; that really smarts. Most likely actually hitting people (or anything that will leave a mark) is going to be off-limits, but don't think for a moment that physical intimidation is something you should avoid. Far from it. Pushing, shoving, jostling, shaking, prodding and tripping are all good ways of increasing your dragon-like status. Just be sure that whatever you do can't be proved, i.e. it's your word against theirs.

> Only hit people if you can be sure no one else will ever find out.

6. **Spit some:** most people try and avoid spitting at others. This is a mistake when you are trying to nurture your full Terribleness. When you know you need to do some berating, try eating a handful of nuts just beforehand.

That plus plenty of water and you'll be spattering them from close range with an unpleasantly chunky mixture.

7. **Be big:** it is important to dominate the physical space in the room. Getting bigger will help you to do this. For men, it is hard to get taller. Female Terrible leaders have a major advantage here through the use of stupendously high heels.

    > A substantial pair of buttocks never did any Terrible leader any harm.

    Everyone can put weight on, perhaps not to the point of being morbidly obese, but certainly to the point of being substantial. This helps should someone 'accidentally walk into you'. Think big clothes, big desk, big car, big dog and big hair. A substantial pair of buttocks never did any Terrible leader any harm either.

8. **Be dramatic:** sudden bursts of anger work well, the more unpredictable the better. Throwing things dramatically across the room also underlines your fearsomeness. If someone has done a lousy piece of work, make sure you print it out so that you can screw it up or rip it up in front of them. Have a few cheap glass objects in your office that you can aggressively sweep off your desk to smash against the wall.

9. **Be red:** try holding your breath in order to pump blood into the capillaries in your face. This will turn you red, making you look more impressive and dreadful. It's best if you do this before the person you want to dragon-ise arrives in your office. It just looks strange if you do this in front of them...

If you can follow these instructions carefully you will find that before long, your own inner dragon is all you need to whip up your staff into a suitable level of panic-induced activity. People often forget this but the most important tool in your Terrible toolbox is, very simply, **you**. You are all you need to create a real sense of fear amongst your people. But ask yourself this: what is more scary than a dragon? That's right — *lots of dragons*. Whether you are finding your own inner dragon hard to really get going, or if your peers are already dragon-like and you need to stand out from the crowd, there are other dragons you can invoke.

True Terrible leaders are wise not to rely on a single-dragon strategy, when a multi-dragon strategy brings the benefits of sustainability and no quarter for your terrified minions. As well as your own inner dragon, I would recommend you are regularly invoking at least two others in order to sustain the peak performance of your people. This is the Terrible law of 'three dragons'.

> True Terrible leaders are wise not to rely on a single-dragon strategy, when a multi-dragon strategy brings the benefits of sustainability.

One of the best dragons to invoke is the external dragon, namely **the competition**. Now, the reality is that your competition is probably a little more accomplished or capable than you are, but this isn't really the point. Read any Dogbert Management book (they are excellent by the way, although they don't take themselves anything like seriously enough given the wisdom they divulge) and you will find advice similar to this. You need to make your competition look fearsome and all-powerful. Tell stories about how great they are, and about all the business you are losing to them. Wax lyrical about the capability of their sales teams and the quality of their research facilities. Make a few redundancies and blame it on the rising power and effectiveness of your competitors. Make it clear that this competitor (be specific — use a named company) is out to kill you. This is a case of them or us, there just isn't room in the market for both companies. Make it out as though this company is maliciously targeting your accounts, and definitely suggest (regardless of whether it is true) that they are using underhand tactics to do so. You need to demonise this organisation, or rather, dragon-ise them. You may need to be a little bit creative to get this done, so invent some stories. Use the template below to really send shivers down the spines of your employees...

"I was talking to an old contact of mine in the pub the other night, you remember Johnnie P? He retired a few years back. He was asked by (insert name of company to be dragon-ised) to do some consulting for them. He got in early one morning and was working in one of their offices. At 9am everyone disappeared into the boardroom, and he wasn't invited to join them. He was fascinated as to what they were up to and so crept in at the back of the room when no one was looking. They had a flag with our logo on it and a life-size doll of our CEO. Each person was asked onto the stage to stick a knife into this

doll. There was chanting and they burned the flag after ceremonially urinating on it. They projected images of us onto a wall and somehow, presumably through the illicit use of social networking sites, they also had images of our families. They called upon some dark spirit to bring down pestilence and disease on all of us. Johnnie P. crept back out and ran away at that point. He was a nervous wreck when I saw him. Now we need to talk about redoubling our efforts, and I'm thinking about cancelling everyone's holiday while I go on a fact-finding mission to Jamaica to learn how to counter-act voodoo curses..."

This should have the desired effect. If you work in the public sector, you might be thinking, "How can I make this dragon work for me?" Fear not. It is a misconception that competition exists only in the private sector, whereas in reality, it is alive and well in all walks of public service. There is always another department out there with ambitions to take over your area, or a charitable organisation that is encroaching on your territory. So, regardless of whether you work in a bank or a hospital, the dragon of the external competitor is a great one to invoke. But by the Terrible law of three dragons, you are going to need at least one more...

"If I have seen farther than others it is because I have stood on the shoulders of giants". So said Sir Isaac Newton, and how right he was. To find your third dragon, look up. A boss, or better still a boss's boss, makes an excellent dragon. Now, they

might in reality be a spineless weasel who only got the job through some family connection, but don't let that dispirit you, in fact this is even better. If they really are a dragon, and a Terrible leader too, then you can simply point out what your minions know to be true, if they step out of line then they'll get it in the neck. If they're a Sissy, you are in a perfect position. You can build them up to look like a dragon and then slay them in front of your minions regularly, thus boosting your own dragon-like status.

Let's assume you're dealing with a Sissy (most likely). You need to start dropping hints and telling stories about their extreme dragon-like qualities. Try dropping these hints in front of the least discreet people in your office. Any of the following should do:

- You saw them break someone's nose with an ashtray when they lost a key account to a competitor. They then bullied witnesses to say at the tribunal that it was them who was assaulted by the other person, and they used the ashtray in self-defence. The other person was later convicted of actual bodily harm and given a three-month jail term.
- They had an affair with their secretary (male or female, doesn't matter). The affair ended unhappily and the secretary threatened to go to a newspaper to tell all. That secretary has never been seen again.
- They have connections with powerful mobsters and corrupt police chiefs who are paid hefty bribes in order to help them keep people quiet.

- You have seen them phone the wife of one of their senior directors in a meeting to ask her if he is normally this 'd***less' or whether he saves up his best efforts for the workplace.

Now that you have created the impression of extreme dragon-like-ness, you need to do something about the reality of their puny and Sissy appearance. You will need to be a bit sly here. Explain to them that your department needs a bit of a kick up the bum, and that you'd really appreciate it if they'd read them the riot act a bit, nothing extreme, just something to stir them to action, perhaps even provide them with a few pointers on an email. Then set up an all-hands meeting for your department or team and invite the Sissy senior manager to talk at it. Let it slip beforehand that the Sissy leader had wanted to tear shreds off the team, but that you had managed to talk them down to giving something more motivational. Your people will be impressed with your ability to talk them down, and intimidated by something that was supposed to be 'motivational', but was in fact quite strongly worded. In this way, you can create your third dragon. Surrounded by fire-breathing behemoths who on regular occasions take big bites out of people, your minions won't know when to stop working they'll be in such a panic. You will have an overtime record Sissy managers can only dream of. And if your company traditionally pays for overtime (a foolish and unnecessary arrangement), you can simply use your dragons as a way of justifying not doing so.

Now, it is possible that one of the dragons above might not work for you all of the time. You might not have a credible external competitor (e.g. you work in NASA) or you might be the CEO and can't invoke a more senior dragon. In which case, have a look at some other potential dragons you could work with:

> **Surrounded by fire-breathing behemoths who on regular occasions take big bites out of people, your minions won't know when to stop working they'll be in such a panic.**

- **Change and redundancy:** we are going back here to Chapter 2 and our lessons on uncertainty. This is an especially poignant dragon in a declining market and you can keep the dragon alive and wreathed in fire and brimstone through regular rounds of organisational restructuring.
- **Fear of failure:** a subtle one this one, but you can use people's own internal dragons as useful motivators. This is a one-to-one approach to be used with particularly troublesome individuals. Get them thinking about their own under-achievement on a daily basis and see if that works to pep them up a bit.
- **Pay cuts:** either as a freeze in pay or as an actual reduction in salary, this can work as a remarkably effective way of encouraging people to redouble their efforts.

Hopefully, you are now beginning to see that the range of dragons available to you is significant. But remember, the most important dragon is you. You can't be all sweetness and light yourself while invoking dragons left, right and centre, so your own inner dragon should be your focus. Some Sissy leaders may say that to focus only on dragons is very negative, and that instead we should try and create desirable, motivating things for our people to move towards. By now, you will be alert to this kind of soft-mindedness. If they had their way, they would create an ill-defined princess, hide her in a dense, metaphorical forest and watch their people struggle to co-ordinate their efforts to find her. We are actually more understanding, results-oriented leaders. We appreciate the mind-bending ineptitude of our cretinous minions. Instead of letting our people struggle away in that forest we create clear, well-articulated and formidably formulated dragons. These dragons make it very clear and simple for our people to understand what they need to do in order to stay alive. We don't expect our people to be sensibly proactive in the search for princesses, but instead, we expect them to be frantically reactive in the avoidance of dragons. We do this because we care. We care about our promotion, our financial success and kicking the sorry butts of the Sissy leaders. But chiefly we do this because we understand human behaviour and we know that you can't rely on people to make sensible decisions about the work they do. People are lazy and feckless and so we need to create the right incentive structure to ensure that things get done. Fast.

In Chapter 7, we looked at how to ensure that the people who work for you never overthrow you. We achieved that through making them miserable. One of the potential drawbacks of making them miserable is a certain lack of vigour that can result from having absolutely no sense of engagement in the work you do. As Terrible leaders, we don't panic if our people look ill-disposed to work

> People are lazy and feckless and so we need to create the right incentive structure to ensure that things get done. Fast.

hard for us, we just tinker with the motivational framework of our organisation. This chapter has been all about how we can do that to the best possible effect, and I hope by now that you will appreciate that even the most organisationally isolated, suicidal, depressed and useless employee can be invoked to significant effort towards your next big promotion. Remember the two following Terrible truths about motivation and you won't go far wrong:

1. The best carrot is actually the absence of the best stick. Formulate the perfect stick (think Worker, Softie, Slick), threaten to use it and watch performance rocket.
2. Sticks work better than carrots. Focus on dragons and ignore princesses. Remember the law of three dragons.

Chapter 7 and Chapter 8 of this book, if deftly combined, will ensure you have a team of mindless, unthreatening minions working frantically for your future glory. You couldn't ask for much more than that, could you!?

Or could you?

Chapter Eight — Lessons in Terrible

- Terrible leaders balance grinding their employees' morale into the dust with maintaining a frenetic level of well-targeted activity.
- In the game of carrot and stick, stick always wins. People move away from unpleasantness more quickly than they move towards nice things.
- And the best carrots are the absence of the best sticks. Find out what your employees really like and then threaten to take these things away.
  - Category One: the *workers* like clear targets and challenging goals. Threaten to remove any goal they've created and dangle the false carrot of promotion just in front of their noses to create years and years of furious industry.
  - Category Two: the *softies* like team harmony and meaningful relationships (whatever they are). Threaten to set them in competition against each other, work alone or to make some redundancies, and just watch the work rate soar. If that fails, shoot some baby deer.
  - Category Three: the *slicks* like to work on high-profile projects with more senior people. Threaten to consign them to the gulag of

Chapter Eight — Lessons in Terrible

projects or to remove previously conferred 'special' advisor status. Award them meaningless changes to their title to make them feel more senior and executive, give them a bigger pot plant and they'll bust their balls.

- In the land of the dragon and the princess, a valiant prince will do more running around because of the dragon, i.e. the burning platform will inspire more focused activity than the most well-honed of inspiring visions.
- Dragons are rarely called Simon. Or Nodgar.
- To generate truly furious levels of activity, you need at least three dragons to instil the required level of fear and dread in your employees.
- You are the most important dragon you will ever own. Remember the nine lessons for being an effective dragon — Volume, Variation, Swear, Get in people's faces, Get physical, Spit some, Be big, Be dramatic, Be red.
- The competition, your boss, change, redundancies, pay cuts and the fear of failure are all excellent dragons to combine with your own inner dragon.

Chapter Eight — Lessons in Terrible

It is not enough that as Terrible leaders we grind our employees' sense of engagement and self-worth into the mud. This is important, yes, but it is also important to maintain them in a constant state of fear-fuelled and frenzied activity while we do it. To achieve that, you'll need sticks and dragons.

CHAPTER 9
POWER AND ITS ABUSES

There are two types of people in this world. There are the hardworking people who will have read every chapter in this book so far, carefully. These are the same people that hang up their work clothes as soon as they get home, tidy up as they go when they're cooking and make lists of things to do. These are the anal people. Nothing wrong with anal people, plenty of Terrible leaders have been sticklers. Then there are those that jumped to this chapter to get some ideas about how to mess people up. I like you guys, you're optimistic and a bit slapdash.

But there's a problem with this approach and I'm afraid the anal people will be chuckling to themselves when I say this, but if you want to abuse power, first you've got to get it. And if you haven't read the first eight chapters, you're going to struggle to build a sufficiently Terrible power base to abuse to any great extent. So, you optimistic people — time to turn around, head back a few chapters and brush up on your speed reading. To those that have worked hard to get to this point: read on. You are about to enter the darkest, most manipulative realm of the Terrible leader. Because for us deeply Terrible types, it is not enough to grind our organisation's self-esteem down to the lowest possible levels in order to prevent even the thought of rebellion from arising. It is not enough to use psychologically targeted sticks and multiple dragons to generate levels of frenetic, focused activity normally reserved for war time. No. We want more. Having created the perfect environment for our Terrible leadership style, we want to be able to take *full* advantage. Some of you will know what I mean by this and will have an instinct for where this chapter is heading. Some of you might even be abusing the power you have created so far. Others may be shocked by some of the suggestions contained in the following chapter.

> Having created the perfect environment for our Terrible leadership style, we want to be able to take *full* advantage.

This is your inner Sissy making its final stand. Push on, because once you have started practicing some of the lessons here, your inner Sissy will finally be banished once and for all...

First let's turn to the question of money. To begin with, it is likely that you will be paid more than your minions. This is only right and proper. You have a more senior, advanced role, with additional responsibilities, and you were assessed as being more capable than them to carry it out. Yours is the hardest role. All your minions have to do is their own job, whereas you have to go to all the effort described in Chapter 8 to create exactly the right kinds of conditions to encourage their performance. It is only right that your organisation pays you considerably more than it pays them, but shouldn't it go further than this? Surely the people who benefit most from your leadership are your own minions. Remember, Terrible leadership is about getting results and they will bask in your reflected glory as target after target is met and exceeded.

All of the effort and time you put into your Terribleness will be of most direct benefit to you, obviously, but your minions also do well out of the bargain. This will be most obvious when it comes to that time of year when you award bonuses. Because you will have read all of the advice in this book carefully, you will have created record levels of activity. Some of it will have been useless, monotonous busy work aimed at building a gargantuan empire so that you can justify your hugely inflated remuneration package, but much more will have been carefully targeted at achieving results through the merciless psychological manipulation of your gormless minions. The end result is a big bonus pool. What happens next is a series of calculations around who gets what. In organisations led by Sissy leaders these are conducted, people are awarded their bonuses, there is a slightly higher than average background level of champagne drinking and then it's back to business as usual. This system runs on a principle that says: *each individual shall be given a sum of money commensurate to their achievements.*

Now, hopefully, through your new-found Terrible lens you will be able to see the gross unfairness of this situation. The problem lies in this part, *'commensurate to their achievements'*. But whose achievements are we really talking about? The individual might have actually done the heavy lifting but who cracked the whip? Let's return to our lesson on carrot and stick theory: remember, if you need to get someone to do something sticks work better than carrots every time. The bonus acts as the carrot in this instance, a single point in the year the employee has to look forward to. You, on the other hand, have been providing the carefully crafted stick all year long, beating them mercilessly and regularly in order to drive optimum performance. Is it fair that they should take home all of their bonus, when if it weren't for you they probably wouldn't have got one at all? The bonus probably only drives around 10–20% of their efforts, whereas your sterling work will have driven much more. It seems only right then in the world of the Terrible leader that you should be rewarded for this effort. Think of this as a levy or tax on their bonus. Left to their own devices they would probably have missed their target and received no bonus at all. With your help and guidance they have smashed their target and therefore stand to gain. Arguably, they should want to give you all of their bonus as a way of demonstrating respect and gratitude to you. Few employees seem to think this is a good idea however, so aim for something a little more modest, around 80% seems appropriate in the circumstances. Extracting 80% of your employees' bonuses should represent a major financial incentive to you, which will drive your own Terribleness to greater heights as this is something only really possible if you have created the right conditions of fear and absolute control. In this way, the organisation stands to gain by this behaviour as more Terribleness means more results — so no one loses out here really, it's a win-win situation. However, extracting 80%

> Is it fair that they should take home all of their bonus, when if it weren't for you they probably wouldn't have got one at all?

of your employees' bonuses is not going to be easy, so here are some hints and tips:

- Don't tell HR: unless they are of a particularly advanced disposition they generally don't go in for this sort of policy, believing instead (and mistakenly) that 100% of an employee's bonus should be paid to them.

- Give employees the option: let them choose whether they would rather receive (A) maximum possible bonus of which they must pay you 80%, or (B) no bonus at all. If they choose A all is well and good. If they choose B sack them on grounds of underperformance. This will be easy to corroborate as the records will show that they received no bonus. In this kind of set-up it is likely that most employees will choose A.

- Keep it unofficial: don't write anything down, and definitely don't let them wander off to the HR department to enquire as to how to re-direct 80% of their bonus to their boss. Instead, arrange to meet them in a disused quarry or factory late at night and have them hand over the money in cash. That way the organisation thinks it is paying bonuses normally and no one will be any the wiser. This subterfuge is also good fun, reinforces the sense of fear and respect your employees will have for you and gives them a night out in some parts of town they probably haven't seen before.

- Take a zero tolerance policy to non-payment: if anyone doesn't show up to hand over the cash or quibbles about the amount, have them kneecapped.

Using this sort of approach, there is no reason why you shouldn't be able to increase your annual earnings by upwards of 50%; more if you work in a bank. But this approach really only covers your direct reports, the people who work directly for you. The more Terrible you become, the more senior you will be and increasingly, you will find a large and complex organisation underneath you. You will not be able to rendezvous with everyone in order to extract their bonuses from them, but fear not, this is not lost revenue to you. You will need a system of bonus levying that stretches across your organisation. As a rule of thumb, aim to have between 40 and 50% of the bonuses of the most junior members of your organisation paid to you in cash in some dark alleyway. This means your direct reports will need to work out how to extract a sufficient amount, without too much being skimmed off in 'handling fees' further down the line. With a large organisation, this should allow your remuneration to increase by several hundred percent, propelling you to retirement, riches and a life of decadence and luxury. This is what I mean by taking *full* advantage — and why not, if you've gone to all that effort to be maximally Terrible, why shouldn't you reap some benefit. However, don't think for a moment that this stops with money, there is much more to abusing power than making yourself rich.

Power is an aphrodisiac. The more Terrible you become, the more powerful you will be and therefore the more irresistible. It doesn't matter if you're 55, overweight, ugly, sweaty and with questionable personal hygiene; in your minion's eyes you have become a demigod. And mere mortals dream of sleeping with the gods. This is not so much an opportunity made possible by dint of Terribleness but an obligation to elevate your minions to levels of godliness only made possible through close personal communion with someone as powerful and fearsome as you are. See this as a task, just one which you are more than happy to conduct meticulously and thoroughly. Once again, those pesky HR whingers won't see this in the same light as you do, and you need to be careful to avoid being labelled as a sexual miscreant. That will do little for your CV or upward career path. So you do need to be delicate and subtle as you set about securing the sexual favours of those within your empire that you desire. In the good old days this was seen as normal, healthy and jolly good fun. The Roman emperor Caligula took the point to the extreme, bedding guests he fancied in between the courses of lavish feasts he threw at his villa. If the ladies' husbands complained, he would simply have them killed. Ah, the good old days! Today we seem to be a little more squeamish about this sort of thing. Whether you are male, female, straight, gay or bi, you need to be just a teeny weeny bit more subtle than Caligula was if you want to avoid an eye-watering number of tribunals.

First, you need to select your target. This should be someone very junior, ideally several levels below you in the management

> It doesn't matter if you're 55, overweight, ugly, sweaty and with questionable personal hygiene; in your minion's eyes you have become a demigod.

hierarchy. Graduates make good targets, as they are young, junior and keen to get ahead. Also, they probably don't have the strong networks in the business that make this sort of thing harder to get away with. Ideally they ought to be bright, keen, enthusiastic, and above all else, naive. We shall call our target Sam, a good gender non-specific name, to make the point that male and female Terrible leaders can play equally well at this game. At a company all hands meeting or away day, make a point of introducing yourself to Sam and being warm, friendly and inviting, welcoming them to the team and finding out how they are enjoying life in the department. They will of course be absolutely terrified, as your Terrible reputation will precede you. Aim to leave Sam with the impression that whatever everyone else might say, as far as they're concerned, you're a really nice person. Leave Sam thinking that perhaps there is something special about them which soothes your Terrible tendencies. Your next job is to work out what they do and what they're interested in. Demonstrating this level of interest in an employee will of course feel strange and unnatural to you, and quite rightly so. However, all you need to find out is the bare minimum about Sam so that later you can create the right type of project to get them involved in. Shake Sam warmly by the hand and express the hope to work with them again soon before heading off to berate some managers far more senior than your protégé within their earshot.

Sam will walk away from this encounter tingling with excitement. "The old dragon's not so bad", they'll say to raised eyebrows from their colleagues. Smile and nod whenever you see them — a careful conspiratorial wink won't hurt either. Sam will by now be harbouring the distinct impression that you are really a very good, kind leader but surrounded by idiots and

> Demonstrating this level of interest in an employee will of course feel strange and unnatural to you, and quite rightly so.

nincompoops. Now your next job is to concoct some trivial, but grandly titled special project that you need some help with. This should be diagnostic rather than applicable in order to prevent Sam from messing up something significant. Drop a few hints to your direct reports that this is something you are interested in, but don't make any specific requests. By now they will be so used to you directing their every move they will not provide you with anything proactively, so it will seem reasonable when, after a few weeks, you have a proper rant at them complaining no one ever listens to anything you want and declare that you are going to assign a 'bright young thing' to a special project to look at 'how we do things round here'. Suggest that this bright young thing will give your established direct reports a 'run for their money'. You have now created the perfect environment into which to lure your target. Sam will be unloved, unsupported and disconnected from the other people who work directly with you, so they will turn to you and only you for support and succour. The trap is set.

Now you need to reach down into your organisational hierarchy to Sam's direct manager. Ideally, this person is themselves a couple of levels below you. Ask them to join you for lunch and engage them in a conversation about this project and its outcomes. Describe your frustration about not having anyone around with a fresh pair eyes to look at the problem. Explain that you would ask them to look at it, but that they are too critical in their current role. If only they had someone in their team they could ask. Explain that you met a bright young spark at some conference recently whose name was Sam. Sam seemed like the sort of person who could do this — did they happen to work for them? Of course at this point the manager will see a connection between the project and some dim recollection of Sam expressing interest in something similar. It seems a perfect match! You express your gratitude for their help by making sure that Sam is back-filled with a good quality person and making sure a small bonus is fed down to their pay packet. Sam is now yours to do with as you please....

Obviously you know that the project you have assigned Sam to is complete rubbish, but Sam doesn't know this. Good projects are things like:

- Overhauling our expenses systems.
- Analysing root causes of poor customer satisfaction ratings.
- What to do about timesheets.
- Network infrastructure strategy.

These are all things no one really cares about, but will give them lots of long, incoherent and rambling conversations to have with various prickly stakeholders. Give Sam a generous three months to dig around and see what they can find out in order to report back to you privately. Have them sit near your office so that they can see and hear the Terrible deeds you indulge in. They still need to see you being Terrible to others and then contrast this by being sweetness and light personified to them. Because you have already created a less than ideal situation for Sam to be working in they will find that their stakeholder interviews are hard work and discouraging, with many of the more senior managers in the department expressing open animosity towards them. They will feel isolated, confused and worried. They will also appreciate that you are very, very busy and may only be able to see them right at the end of the day, perhaps at around 7pm. At this point suggest taking the meeting to the bar or pub in order to have a drink too. Reassure them that they are doing a good job and listen attentively to their idiotic insights, nodding and smiling all the time. Ask them for suggestions as to what could be done differently and make a few notes or very brief calls to people to begin generating some actions (these can always be countermanded later). By 8pm, you and Sam will be hungry and rather than heading off to your respective homes suggest you grab a quick bite on the way through. They will be thrilled by your invitation. It is now that a little forethought will have been required...

Earlier in the week you will have booked a table at a very exclusive and expensive restaurant, ideally one where they know you. At 8pm, ask Sam if they like French food and then say you'll see if you can get a table at this Michelin-starred place round the corner. Pretend you are phoning to see if you can get a table, whereas in reality you already have one. Whisk Sam off to said restaurant and, to be honest, if you need hand holding with what to do next, I despair. Just order plenty of wine and make sure your husband or wife (if you have one) thinks you're at some conference.

Now the trick with Sam is knowing when to end the relationship. A couple of months is all you will want to maintain something like this for. The novelty will wear off and then you'll want to move onto pastures new. If Sam shows any signs of getting difficult or uppity, then end the relationship immediately. Of course, ending the relationship also means terminating Sam's employment with the organisation. It is dangerous to have ex-Sams wandering around your organisation. Everyone else will forget about Sam very quickly, but not if Sam is still hanging around. Also, once you have a Sam 'build up' it becomes embarrassing and awkward; imagine having eight or 10 of them in the organisation. It becomes a little obvious. No, you'll need to dispose of your Sams once they become stale and uninteresting, and you'll need to contain yourself to no more than a couple of Sams per year, otherwise you run the risk of being found out...

> You'll need to dispose of your Sams once they become stale and uninteresting.

So, we've looked at how to extract a decent percentage of your employees' bonuses into your own bank account, and we've worked out how to use your power and Terribleness to get your Sams into bed. Is there anything else we can do to abuse the mountain of power you have carefully accrued? Of course there is...

An obvious abuse of your new-found power is the corporate expenses system. This is normally used to book flights, hotels, train tickets, conferences etc. associated with normal business life. However, these systems work just as well for booking holidays, building works on your house, nights out for your friends and family etc. In order to do this, the first thing you will need to establish is whether your boss is going to scrutinise your or your department's expenses. If they're not, then you've got a lot less work to do, but if they are, don't lose heart, there is still much you can do here. If your boss is a stickler who wants to sign off all the expenses then, in some way, this actually helps, because anything they do sign off will be assumed to be squeaky clean and no one else would think to challenge it. To get this done well you need some equipment:

• A fall guy — someone with whom to collaborate, and who, if it comes to it, will take the heat.
• A spurious and expensive project.
• An administrator you can bribe.

Set up a 'special projects' team. This could be led by a high-profile team member who seems credible enough, but feel free to pack out the team with the biggest bunch of losers and cretins you can gather together. Give them the job of 'developing corporate strategy' or something similarly meaningless and then get them flying around the world, either to visit colleagues in other countries, or if you don't have any, to visit the installations of other organisations to see how they do things in emerging markets. You need to establish a healthy, regular and high level of spend on flights to exotic locations. Explain to the head of this team that you want to join them on some of these trips. You can always make up some rubbish like, 'overseeing for quality or research purposes'.

Now you have a background situation rumbling away that will facilitate a bit of liberal expense account abuse. All you need now is an administrator who you can bribe and you're on your way to a lot of free luxurious holidays for you and your family (or you could always take Sam along instead...). Finding the right administrator shouldn't be too hard, it is a question of identifying the right kind of leverage. Watch out for any of the following:

- A PA or administrator being dismissed for poor conduct by a member of your management team, you can swoop in, be their saviour and then ask them for a few favours...
- A PA or administrator who is clearly bone idle, lazy or up to no good — these are like gold dust and can be used for all of these slightly shadowy tasks...
- A PA or administrator who is having an affair with another member of staff, but who already has a wife/husband and kids at home, i.e. someone with lots of leverage...
- And if you catch an administrator fiddling their expense account...! You have just struck the jackpot...

You need this administrator to help you book the flights and the holidays using the expense system. Because you are a senior Terrible leader it is beneath you to undertake administrative tasks, nefarious or otherwise. And if you're honest with yourself, do you really

> All you need now is an administrator who you can bribe and you're on your way to a lot of free luxurious holidays for you and your family.

understand how to use the wretched system? No, I didn't think so. Make sure the administrator gets some small perk or kickback as a result of providing you with this service, and if they show any sign of blabbing sack them with lightning fast reflexes.

So, there you have your perfect set-up for abusing the expenses system. But — don't forget your fall guy —— Terrible leaders never do anything without a back-up plan. If your boss, or their boss or some meddlesome grunt somewhere else in the organisation looks into the monstrously inflated expense bill being generated by your department, you will need a degree of 'plausible deniability' in order to emerge unscathed. Indeed, as ever with Terrible leadership, getting found out just gives you a new opportunity.

> Because you are a senior Terrible leader it is beneath you to undertake administrative tasks, nefarious or otherwise.

If the whistle is blown, you quickly move to deny all knowledge of this horrific abuse of the company's expense budget. Your fall-guy is quickly identified as running an irresponsibly badly-managed budget, removed from the organisation, along with everyone connected with the project. You will be applauded by your bosses for such quick and determined action, and your other minions will quake in their shoes at such ruthless beheadings. You then launch a special project looking into the department's expense policy and procedure. Now, if only there was some bright young thing to look into the situation with a fresh pair of eyes...

Remember: Terrible leaders never panic. It isn't seemly and it certainly does nothing to improve your Terrible reputation. Being Terrible gives you a whole new angle with which to play the organisation, the business world and your feckless minions. With Terribleness, when it's good it's good, and when it's bad it's better. What I tend to find is that in the middle of most piles of shit there is a speck of gold. It's just that most people don't have the inclination to look for it...

> In the middle of most piles of shit there is a speck of gold. It's just that most people don't have the inclination to look for it.

So, we've cornered the bonus market, we've lured the graduate population to our boudoirs and we've horribly abused our expenses system. Yet, there is much more we can do in order to extract full value from your investment in Terribleness. We have already seen how as your Terribleness increases so will your seniority and position within the organisation. This will put you in charge of increasingly large budgets to spend on procuring contracts and services from third-party suppliers. This is a tough job in an increasingly competitive world full of multiple suppliers who can all basically provide similar levels of service.

As Terrible leaders, we should see straightaway that this gives us an opportunity to extract some value from the situation. After all, it is only fair that these suppliers, who have everything to gain and nothing to lose, should provide you with a number of services to facilitate your decision-making process. I'd advise you make it known to them subtly that any of the following would work:

- Days out at prestigious sporting events.
- Gifts of wine, holidays, yachts, cars or cash.
- Nights out in strip clubs.
- Opportunities to meet high-ranking politicians.

Watch them crawl over each other to fill your life with all the best things (the best things in life are free apparently). Once you have awarded one contract on the basis of a heavy bribe, the word will be out there and you can just watch the gifts come pouring in. This situation is, however, somewhat unsustainable and the gifts only conferred at those times when there is a contract to be awarded. If you want to 'push the envelope' (awful Sissy phrase), you could think about awarding contracts based on the supplier paying you a monthly kickback based on a percentage of the contract value. Even if you could encourage suppliers to pay you personally as little as 2–3% of the value of the contracts you award, this can get considerable once you start managing multi-million pound budgets.

> Once you have awarded one contract on the basis of a heavy bribe, the word will be out there and you can just watch the gifts come pouring in.

You need to keep all of these payments and gifts to a reasonable background level. This will depend on the culture of the country you work in. If you work in a strongly Sissy-inspired culture (like Sweden) you will need to be very careful indeed. If you work in West Africa, then happy days.

The trick is to secure these payments and gifts for the *long term*. Far better to have a small percentage of contract values paid to you over many years (a level which the contractor will bear without going bust) than a large percentage that is sniffed out by some busybody in the first six months. Remember our example of Hitler. He achieved a lot and he was definitely Terrible, but he got too ambitious too quickly and, as a result, people spotted the fact that he was trying to take over the world. Never let people see too much of your ambition. Your Terribleness needs to be like an iceberg. The bit above the water line is your visible Terribleness. It is terrible indeed to behold, jagged, frightening and people learn quickly that if you run up against it you get big holes torn in your side and you sink.

But there is much more to your Terribleness than just that; there is all your craft and subtle skill in creating the perfect environment (see Chapters 7 and 8) for abusing your new-found power. And it's best if people only see so much of this. This is the part that really drives the value in being Terrible, it is the final result, the real reason we set out on this Terrible path. We are Terrible to gain power, and we gain power so that we use and abuse it to get the things we want.

Earlier I said for a Terrible leader if it's good it's good, and if it's bad it's better. This is absolutely true for underperformance. Most Sissy leaders really sweat about the underperformance of their employees. Now, as Terrible leaders we have already seen two reasons why we wouldn't:

1. Underperformers are great for padding out your organisation. They make your empire look bigger without placing any additional demands on your role in terms of identifying useful things for them to do.

2. You rarely suffer much from underperformance as you know how to create the perfect incentive (i.e. threatening people with the most psychologically targeted of sticks) and you have instigated a dread force of three dragons aimed at stirring your minions into frantic, focused activity.

> Underperformers are great for padding out your organisation.

But there is yet a third reason why chronic, mind-numbing underperformance shouldn't worry you. If someone really just hasn't got what it takes and you've tried the sticks and the dragons and you still can't get anything useful from them, think twice before you banish them to the Siberian equivalent of your organisation (Quality Control, Project Management, or HR are always good departments to stash your losers in). Could this person provide a useful function to you in some other way? If they're as useless as you think they are, then they probably wouldn't get a job anywhere else and they know they wouldn't. You have potential leverage on this useless dolt, and you could use this to your advantage. For this sort of eventuality, it is useful to keep a list of jobs you need to get done but that you don't really want to do yourself. Here's my list that sits in my top drawer at the moment:

1. Crawl down into the sewer under my house and clear out the pipe that keeps getting blocked (too messy).
2. Assassinate anyone associated with 'reality' television (too risky).
3. Fiddle my tax return (too boring).
4. Pick up my dog's poop (too smelly).
5. Set up an office in Mauritania (too out the back of beyond).
6. Charity work (too allergic to sick or poor people).

Our chronic underperformers could come in handy for any of these tasks. Take the last one for example. We'd all like to do more work for charity, it's good for our soul on the off-chance those religious types turn out to be right, and it makes us look generous and interesting and therefore more attractive to the opposite sex. Two good reasons why you should do more for charity. But, obviously, you won't want to put any of your actual personal time towards this sort of thing — no! That's where your chronic underperformers come in. Even they should be able to slap a bit of paint on a wall or tidy up some pensioners' garden. You could even set up a scheme for your department whereby the really genuinely useless are farmed out to local charities on a regular basis. You might have to shave off their pay a little bit to make sure they're not too much of a drain on the organisation, but they'll see this as acceptable as they are essentially now being paid to do what criminals are forced to do in order to avoid prison terms for petty offences. Your immortal soul will get a good rub down and you'll be able to adopt the moral high ground whenever you need to. If they've got a bit of time left over after having picked up litter at the local school, have them pop round and walk your dog. Oh — and while they're at it, are they any good with drainage systems...?

> Your immortal soul will get a good rub down and you'll be able to adopt the moral high ground whenever you need to.

We should spend more time with charities as Terrible leaders. Obviously not for the same reason as Sissy leaders, but consider this: they are generally one of the more tax-efficient vehicles available for the distribution of funds. A useful way to abuse your new-found Terribleness is through the placing of large sums of money into a charitable, low-tax organisation that you can draw on at a later date. Each year, make a habit of making a considerable donation to a worthy charitable cause. In a quiet moment, set up a charity yourself (this is surprisingly easy in most countries) and then channel these funds to that charity. You can then have the charity hold a percentage of these funds in a 'pension fund' that you can draw on in later life. This is a really long-term strategy, and you will need a few ingredients to make this work:

1. All the paperwork of a bonafide charity.

2. An annual report outlining the income and expenditure of the charity.
3. Photos and emails from the grateful disadvantaged recipients of the charities' actions.

All of these can be relatively easily mocked up, although a good accountant, at least a good Terrible accountant, would make the process a lot easier for you. Make sure the photos and letters from the receivers of your charity's good works make their way into prominent places around the office. If people in your department or team make a lot of noise about wanting to go and actually help these people, you might have to occasionally (once every three years or so) bribe a number of homeless people to act out the necessary roles to fully create the illusion of a charitable organisation that is alive and working hard. There is no reason why your charity couldn't be gratefully receiving between 1–3% of your department's profit, maybe even that of your whole organisation with a little bit of salesmanship.

So, we have seen that once you have set up the right Terrible conditions for leadership the opportunities for abusing the broad resulting power base are numerous and extensive. You can extract people's bonuses; you can sleep with the attractive members of your staff; you can work the expenses system to your benefit and have contractors pay you for the privilege to work for your organisation; you can deploy your underperformers to do your dirty work and you can set up spurious charities to siphon off your organisations' profit margin. If you can do even half of these things, you should be very proud of yourself. Simply being able to do some of these things is an indicator in itself that you have grown truly Terrible, but not only that; you are revelling in and enjoying your Terribleness to the full.

For you the path to Terribleness is showering you with the hard-earned fruits of the conqueror. Terribleness is not bringing fringe benefits; Terribleness is now bringing returns 10 or 20 times greater than Sissy leadership would have done. You will now look at your Sissy colleagues and see them for the snivelling, weak-minded fools they are, struggling through meaningless lives unfulfilled and unrewarded. Rise up to your full height, look down on them in scorn and think about your next abuse of power. Here are some quick ones you might want to think about:

> You will now look at your Sissy colleagues and see them for the snivelling, weak-minded fools they are.

1. Have people pay you for giving them overtime shifts. This practice is common on most major building sites where the foreman will take a bribe for giving his friends the pick of the overtime shifts. This is particularly good if you are still a relatively junior Terrible leader. Try and create an open market rather than a set price so that people always have the opportunity to outbid each other.

2. Do a deal with a recruitment agency. They typically get a percentage of the first year's salary of each candidate they place. If you make it easy for them to place lots of

candidates in your organisation (at the same time making your empire look awesome), it seems only fair that they recognise your generosity.

3. Do less work. Now that you have your organisation humming, it seems only reasonable that you can dedicate more time to important executive pursuits such as the spa, golf, exotic holidays etc. Thanks to advances in technology it is now just as easy to berate your useless employees from the golf course as it is from the boardroom.

If these seem too basic, then there are more advanced forms of Terribleness that are particularly profitable that you can get involved in if your organisational set up allows you to do so. For example, if your company has a logistics arm that you are in charge of, have you considered human trafficking? This works well whether it's whole humans you are moving from A to B, or just parts of humans for organ transplant. Now, in most parts of the world, this sort of activity is illegal, or at least frowned upon by the authorities so there is some risk involved. You'll need someone to pin the blame on and some well-bribed people in positions of power, but you should only consider courses of action like this if you have already fully extended yourself in your own organisation. Narcotics, conflict diamonds, forged banknotes, exotic animals (dead or alive) and depleted uranium also all make excellent items to think about moving around the world under the control of a truly Terrible leader. Again, most of these are not strictly 'legal' so there will be inherently more risk involved in getting involved in this kind of stuff, but consequently higher levels of reward. Certainly, it's worth considering...

Hopefully, through the course of this chapter, you will have seen that Sissy leaders think far too one-dimensionally about their roles in organisations. You don't just have a job to do. You have a position to abuse. The success and extent to which that abuse can be brought to full expression depends on the degree of Terribleness you are able to exert on your minions and the wider organisational system. Get this right and a job that usually pays $100,000 should mean a take home of $1 million or more. Given how much effort you will have put into your Terribleness, the degree of effort you have put into turning yourself into a dragon-esque scourge of the department, doesn't it seem

> You don't just have a job to do. You have a position to abuse.

perverse to *not* make the most of the situation? You have to ask yourself this: what is the point of acquiring power? For the sake of power in itself? That would make you a pretty shallow and unattractive sort of a person. No, power itself is not the true aim of Terribleness, it is what power bestows, what power brings to those brave enough and strong enough to wield it wisely and ruthlessly. Most of your fellow citizens do not have this power and cannot see past what having it would mean. Those of us who attain it use it as a shield. Let people think it is the power itself that motivates and drives us. We are really playing a larger and more Terrible game, one they cannot see most of the time and that suits us fine. Society will label you as ambitious and power-hungry. Grasp the label, hold it dear to you and use it to mask what you truly intend until it suits you to reveal your true scheme. As your minions gratefully hand you 80% of their annual bonus and watch you climb back into the Bentley you bought on expenses and whisk Sam off to a romantic rendezvous in a Michelin-starred restaurant, they will realise that it might not have just been the power you were after. It was much, much more...

Chapter Nine — Lessons in Terrible

- Now that you've attained a Terrible reputation and the resultant fear and respect that is due to you, *use it!*
- Ask yourself not what you can do for your people, but how much of their bonus should they give to you? After all, they are only being awarded a bonus because of your well-honed and masterful motivational techniques, so doesn't it belong to you in the first place?
- Not getting enough of the bad thing at home? Screw the graduates, or anyone else who tickles your fancy. But remember, after you've got them in the sack, to give them the sack shortly afterwards.

Chapter Nine — Lessons in Terrible

- The company expenses system is a gold mine in the right hands. It is worth setting up a mining team.
- Make sure suppliers know you're bribe-able. Then think long term.
- Use your truly useless employees to do the things you don't want to. They won't complain, and if they do, they are the easiest to fire on grounds of gross incompetence.
- Get involved in charities. They are a great place to siphon company funds into for a rainy day.
- Think about every angle to extract value from your position: take payments for awarding overtime; do a deal with a recruitment agency and then make loads of personnel changes; just work less and make others do your work for you.
- Think about human trafficking if this all seems a bit too mundane...

Being a Terrible leader is a tough job, and while well paid, especially if you work in a bank, it is almost certainly not well paid enough. By abusing the power you have attained, you can make being Terrible pay properly.

part four

Terrible within a modern organisational setting

I need to check you are awake. If you have a notepad with a 'to do' list that reads something along the lines of 'abuse expenses system', 'abuse graduates', 'steal staff bonuses', 'buy rice', ...then we have a problem. The previous three chapters are the exact opposite of a useful manual for leading your people. The topics covered are absolutely crucial to effective leadership, but of course the treatment given by the Terrible leader is all about-face. Reading these chapters, we come back to a fundamental truth about leadership: we are here to create meaningful lives for the people we lead. If we get it wrong, the best we can hope for is activity without engagement; a dull, senseless, reactive plodding through our working days without considered thought or motivation. If we get it right, we create a meaningful connection between our people and what occupies their time at work.

To achieve this the 4Es discussed in Chapter 7 are of course vital. Empowerment is talked about a lot in organisations around the world, the feeling being that hierarchical organisational structures are, in many places, outdated and inefficient. Empowerment is the desire to give more self-direction to our people, which, if you work in an industry where people take complex decisions about what they are going to focus on and how, will be critical if you are to get anything like a decent level of productivity. Empowerment is a tricky cake to bake however, and certainly isn't a discrete concept, comprising at least three separate elements for leaders to master. First, you must create a level of crystal clarity as to the specific nature of people's goals and the expectations of their role. Second, they need to have the skills and capabilities required to achieve those goals. Finally, they need a degree of self-belief and confidence that they can achieve those goals, with the space and time required to make their decisions.

Creating a sense of empowerment is your responsibility. It won't build itself, and you will find it surprisingly easy to break by stepping in and making decisions about everything all of the time. Equally, it is your responsibility to be empathic, build a sense of energy and to help your people engage fully with the work they are doing. One of the great transitions for us as leaders is to step away and drop our constant obsession with targets and goals, i.e. the work that the team does. This is still important, but so is the team itself, its level of capability, engagement and empowerment. The team can handle the work itself, but no one is going to attend to the innate level of energy within the team. Apart from you.

Once you have created those conditions, the next challenge for many of us is that not all individuals respond to the same thing in the same way. The nature of individual differences means that, despite our best efforts to create an empowering work environment, it might not work in the same way for everyone. That's where Chapter 8 comes in. Whereas the Terrible leader is interested in using motivational insights to create a series of threats by removing aspects of people's working lives that they find inherently motivational, we can use the same insight to identify what really works for people. The great truth in this chapter is that people are not motivated simply by what motivates you! Many leaders attempt to motivate their people using the same things that work for themselves. This will work for around 30–40% of people, but the rest will find your approach somewhat lacking. This realisation is vital if you are going to appeal as a leader to all kinds of people. And you need all kinds of people. It doesn't matter if you work in an investment bank or a children's hospital, you need 'workers', 'softies' and 'slicks' in every walk of life or you will find the workplace becomes a very lopsided and risk-prone place where major issues, risks or opportunities go completely unrealised. I would encourage you to think carefully about your own team. What kind of people are they? How do you motivate them? Are you differentiating your style sufficiently?

The rest of Chapter 8 is more tricky to strictly reverse. When we talk about dragons and princesses up to a point this is absolutely true, you do need to be able to articulate a clear dragon (or burning platform) if you are going to motivate people towards change. But it is dangerous in the extreme to ignore the princess. The best change is the change we move towards, not move away from. The change we choose is better than the change we have inflicted upon us. So working with your team, you will need to identify the goal, the vision, the thing you are united in striving for. This needs to be something that is intrinsically and genuinely attractive to you all. And as for spitting at people...

Chapter 9 was a lot of fun to write, but there is a serious point. Many leaders have fallen into the traps illustrated in Chapter 9, and if you ever get even close to falling in one, you need to be very careful indeed. Once you have abused your position, you run a very significant risk of being found out, and once found out, you run the risk of your entire career ending up in tatters. Many leaders and politicians have discovered exactly that. In the UK, we have been surrounded for over a year now (I write this in early 2011) with ministers abusing their expenses. Many have lost their jobs and had their entire reputations tarnished as a result. What's interesting is that very few of them, perhaps none of them, will have set out with Terrible intentions. We get dragged into these traps insidiously, slowly and sometimes without fully realising it. Are we abusing our power or being pragmatic? Are we abusing our power or falling in love? Are we abusing our power or enjoying some time with friends who just happen to be suppliers? From our point of view, it's pretty easy to see how we'd like to interpret the situation. But it's not our point of view we should worry about. Ask yourself, how would this look to someone else in a few years' time if you were trying to explain things out of context? Would it stack up then?

Ok, health warning over. Remember, you're a good, well intentioned person. But that doesn't stop the Terrible leader getting up to more mischief...

CHAPTER 10
PUSHING HR OVER THE EDGE

Ivan, Vlad, Stalin, Marcos and Genghis Khan all had something in common. They didn't have to worry about the idiots in the HR department. And the similarities don't stop there. With the exception of Stalin, they passed on their realms to their family (or at least they planned to). The world has changed since the times of our heroes, and Terrible leadership must therefore adapt accordingly. We now have legal frameworks to work around, and policies to spot loopholes in. Nepotism, for so long a positive force in our world, is going through a frowned upon phase. Our Terribleness must respond to the environment of the 21st Century and the rest of this book is dedicated to making sure that your historical appreciation of classical Terribleness, combined with your finely-honed Terrible capabilities, are not blunted by the modern world's Sissiness.

I assume that if you are reading beyond this point, you have either attained a frightening level of Terribleness, or you have every intention of doing so. Let it not be washed away by the peculiarities of our time, but instead use the learning of the next two chapters to adapt it to fit in.

When going into battle, the first and most important thing that you need to be able to do is to recognise your enemy. It was widely reported in the press in 2010 that the Russian army were deploying a range of lifelike, inflatable military ordnance. Everything from tanks to mobile radar stations in rubber inflatable form. These inflatables were not some cheap children's bouncy castle mock-up, but high-tech pieces of equipment treated with chemicals to trick radar and heat-sensing equipment. Clever, clever Russians, Ivan would be very proud. They know, as does every little critter that uses camouflage to evade getting ripped to pieces by bigger critters, that evading detection is the first step in winning the battle. As Terrible leaders, you have several advantages over everyone else when it comes to winning in the corporate environment:

1. Firstly, you have learnt to relish combat. Rather than something to avoid you have learnt to see combat for what it really is: an opportunity to get ahead. It is said, possibly apocryphally, that telemetry from Formula 1 racing cars illustrates an interesting phenomenon that distinguishes the very best drivers from the also-rans. When most drivers see a crash happening ahead of them they brake, or at least they ease off the accelerator. But not the very best drivers. The world champions actually accelerate into this uncertainty, and so should you. Combat is to be welcomed, as with it almost certainly comes new opportunities.

2. Secondly, you have become good at conflict, it gives you an opportunity to unleash your inner dragon, to soar to majestic heights and decapitate people at will.

3. Thirdly, you actually *see* the conflict. Many people make

the mistake of seeing the world of work as a collaborative situation where we all work together to build rainbows and ice-cream and other frilly nonsense. Fortunately, you see the world for the squalid struggle that it really is and have learnt how to come out on top. So, you should feel supreme confidence in engaging with enemies of any type or distinction, and indeed relish this experience. But who are these enemies?

> You see the world for the squalid struggle that it really is and have learnt how to come out on top.

Your first and most obvious enemy are the minions that work for you. We've already looked in detail at how to ensure they do not bring about your downfall. You should take this threat seriously and move quickly to minimise it.

But there is another serious combatant in the ring and you need to make sure this one doesn't go undetected. They call themselves various things, usually Human Resources, but also sometimes other weird and wonderful titles like, 'The People Team' or 'Organisation Development'. Don't be distracted by the fancy titles, all of these groups are essentially HR, or Personnel in old-timer talk. HR represent a potential thorn in your side. They are the group who look after things like employment law, policy and equality and diversity. I apologise for so much bad language in one sentence, I will try not to spring such a tirade on you again, and I can understand if you are feeling a little queasy at this point. But here's the thing, you need to recognise and understand your enemy before you can mount a successful offensive.

Now beware! HR 'professionals' (if they can be called such) have learnt over long exposure to leaders of all types (including Terrible ones) to be quite chameleon-like in their approach to leaders like you, just like those inflatable Russian tanks. Theirs is a slippery, devious profession. They will attempt to charm you and tell you that everything you're doing is right and proper. They will even adopt a style similar to your own (they call this mirroring, but think of it more like parroting), in an attempt to win you over. Indeed, to a Terrible leader, you may think in your HR person you have found a like-mind, a kindred spirit, someone to collaborate and conspire with. DO NOT BE FOOLED!!! This is exactly what they want you to think. They may be spiky, difficult and boorish on the outside but if you cut open an HR person you will find them stuffed with baby pandas and camomile tea. They might even encourage your innate Terribleness, but be warned, they'll have you strung up in front of an employment tribunal or works council double fast. But why would they behave this way? It does seem illogical but there are some essential things you need to understand about HR.

> They may be spiky, difficult and boorish on the outside but if you cut open an HR person you will find them stuffed with baby pandas and camomile tea.

Firstly, there really is no such job as Human Resources. Think about it, what do they actually *do*? Think harder... and harder.... That's right! Nothing. They are an expensive way for companies to say, "Look we care about our people enough to employ some broadly useless individuals to take care of them". HR is padding. This is a tactic we have explored as Terrible leaders in previous chapters, the idea of padding your organisation with basically useless people in order to make your empire look larger and more impressive. This is a perfectly reasonable strategy and one you will have used yourself. But it gives you a particular challenge with respect to HR. All other groups would leave you well alone to pursue your own Terrible path, but not HR, they have a tendency to get in the way.

Let me give you an example. You may have worked hard to establish a finely honed system of intangible and vague performance targets for your people. HR will want to see these tightened up, which as you know could lead to disastrous consequences. If a new minion dares to question your thinking in a meeting you will naturally want to summarily dismiss them. HR might insist that this cretinous individual is paid to go quietly, or, even worse, might question their leaving altogether. Normally, you would just sack the HR person too, but they may well be a peer and that may well not be possible. Also, if you routinely hack through 10+ HR people a year (a compelling thought I appreciate) you will find yourself under a lot of unwanted scrutiny from further up the organisation.

The fact is HR can be a real nuisance and are one of the very few things that genuinely stands between you and your Terrible fulfilment. This is serious. Reading Chapter 9 will no doubt have alerted you to the significant benefits Terribleness brings. You don't want to let that slip away just because of some weepy, cringing, socialist do-gooder who enjoys relative immunity from your Terrible reflex as a result of their position. This will not do. We need to push these HR types over the edge, and if possible, professionally discredit them in the process if our Terrible future is to be fully realised. In order to defeat this enemy, first we must understand it. What you are about to read will seem at times alarming, irrational and even painful, but I urge you to see the course and read all of it. You need to step into the mindset, into the messed-up and confused world of Human Resources.

Your typical HR person will believe that an organisation's most important resource is its people. I know! Vacuous isn't it, but they really do believe this rubbish. Obviously, the enlightened among us know that an organisation's most expensive and least efficient resource is its people, and that the most important resource is its most gullible customer segment.

> An organisation's most expensive and least efficient resource is its people.

However laughable, it is important to understand this premise as it gives us an insight into some of the more lunatic ideas and priorities of your typical HR nut-job. Because of this skewed lens, they will want to assign a percentage of profits to 'staff training'. This is where they organise to have your useless minions corralled into a room and shown PowerPoint slides with pictures of squirrels on them. Or something like this. It is probably ritualistic and unhealthy and I suggest you avoid 'staff training' at all costs. Now, obviously, the mindless blobs you call 'staff' will not learn anything from this effort, it is just a way of wasting time and money, but the HR team will yammer on about the benefits of this kind of activity until you have an aneurism. This is particularly true if your organisation is involved in heavy engineering, drilling for oil, mining etc, i.e. where there is a significant risk of injury or death if your minions mess stuff up. HR seem to look past the fact that nature has already created a perfectly effective system for dealing with dangerous activities. It is called natural selection and it works by winnowing out the most moronic of your employees who will end up variously scorched, singed, squashed or entombed. The more fleet-footed will survive, the more dim-witted will perish. The system is equitable, reasonable and cheap and as a result clearly leaves no real need for health and safety training. The other problem with training is that, for as long as your direct reports are in training, they are *not* working towards your next promotion and future glory. You have gone to a lot of effort to create the ideal motivational environment for your people, with just the right number of petrifying dragons and threats, so you want to have them working in it as much as possible, not off with some hippy having a love-in, looking at squirrels.

But staff training is not the end to HR's madness. They will also want you to create something called a 'succession plan'. This is not what you imagine it to be. A succession plan would suggest itself to be a plan about how you are going to become successful. This would be a reasonable thing but what the HR loonies are actually talking about (brace yourself here, this is going to hurt) is a plan for who is going to replace you! I appreciate you may have to read that sentence again and that you'll assume I have made some horrific typing error that my editor has failed to pick up. Alas, this is not the case. HR will actually want you to have planned out who is going to replace you from within your own team. They will even want you to be working to develop their skills such that they can replace you ... wait for it ... *more easily*!!!! Unbelievable. It is hard to see any plausible reason for this sort and level of insanity. Here at the Terrible Leadership Research Institute we have looked into why they might want to encourage this so-called 'succession planning'. Apparently it is to, and I quote, 'reduce organisational risk'. I know, it doesn't make any sense why having a plan to replace your immense Terribleness would reduce risk. Surely the real risk is that you leave and go to another organisation, a risk they could mitigate easily enough by giving you a generous increase in your remuneration package.

> When HR start talking about succession plans you need to take firm action.

When HR start talking about succession plans you need to take firm action, which we will come to in a moment but not before we investigate more freakish beliefs of the HR community.

Talent management is another drum the committed HR moron will beat with abandon. Again, you will assume that this would apply to how the organisation goes about managing you. But think again, it actually refers to the identification of 'talent' in your organisation. Now, be careful here. You know full well that there is no talent in your organisation, and that if it weren't for you, nothing would ever get done at all. However, saying this to HR doesn't seem to satisfy them; if anything, it seems to make matters worse and they become even more insistent on doing a 'talent review'. This involves sitting in a room with lots of post-it notes and lists of names and grids. It's all completely pointless, but at our research institute, we found after scrutinising this effort repeatedly that what the HR person is trying to do is identify which of your minions are the least and most useless. I know this sounds crazy, but it gets worse. They will want you to take the ones they identify as having the most potential and develop and promote them. Of course we would never be stupid enough to do such a thing, minions can be dangerous, the last thing you would do is to encourage them to be *more* dangerous. The HR person will also encourage you to 'performance manage' the most useless of your employees. By this they mean fire them, but not in the Terrible meaning of 'fire them'. If they just wanted you to fire them that would be one thing, you could always arrange a hefty kickback with a recruiting agency and set up a good steady revolving door at the front of the office. That could be a good little earner. But what the HR fool actually wants you to do is 'manage them out of the organisation'. This means an interminable series of conversations where you point out to them in sugared terms just how useless they really are before encouraging them to leave the company. Now, as Terrible leaders we completely buy in to the idea of giving feedback. Remember, every mistake is an opportunity to teach someone a lesson. However, if we managed every useless minion out of the organisation there would be no one left! Those useless minions are providing a crucial role: they make you look good. Their chronic ineptitude means you will look, by comparison, even better. Their sheer numbers mean everyone else will assume you are a powerful and influential leader. No, you don't want to manage these people out of the organisation unless it is for Terrible reasons such as creating a little added frisson to people's working lives, or to cheer you up if you are having a bad day.

There is an almost endless stream of HR nonsense I could relay to you, but the last one I will alert you to is equality and diversity. This one is a real worry, and it flies in the face of all common sense. This is a case of political correctness gone insane. If you are reading this book in a country where it is still permissible to fire a woman because she is pregnant, then make the most of it as I fear those days are numbered. Sissy management mantras are spreading through the vector of HR ninnies. Don't say I didn't warn you. This equality and diversity nonsense stipulates that you can't fire someone for being old. You can't fire someone for being young. You can't fire someone for being disabled. You can't fire someone for being white, black, brown, pink or green. You can't fire someone for being a woman, or a man, or somewhere in-between. You can't fire gay people, or straight people. Now, in Terrible leadership terms, these are all perfectly normal, admissible and expedient reasons to end someone's employment. I mean, who else is there!? Point to someone who isn't white, black, brown, pink, green, male, female, straight, gay, old, young or pregnant. Yep, you're pointing at the actuaries aren't you and you have a point, they are completely out of this world, but actuaries aside this equality and diversity nonsense means you can't fire anyone for being anything! Let's imagine you have a female employee who gets pregnant. The obvious step would be to fire them as they are shortly going to become a lot less productive. Let's imagine you have an employee that has a car accident and is left in a wheelchair. It will take them a while to get the hang of life on wheels. Surely they should be doing that on their own time. Let's imagine you have a member of staff who is getting quite old and slowing down. This is surely nature's way of saying, 'fire them now and keep the pension costs down'. In a right-thinking, common sense world this is all straightforward enough.

> Let's imagine you have a female employee who gets pregnant. The obvious step would be to fire them.

If you have some small people living with you it is likely that they are your 'children'. You can tell these people apart from adults not just by their size but by their tendency not to have jobs or to make any serious contribution to the household finances. To find out more about these creatures you will need to read 'Terrible parenting' but I'm not interested in the children, I'm interested in the small, inexpensive pets they seem to accrue. You know the ones I mean: cats, rabbits, hamsters, rats, spiders, crabs etc. If one of these gets ill what do you do? Take it to the vet and spend lots of money on treatments and operations? Of course not, you pop it in a zip-lock plastic bag, seal it and throw it in the river or stamp on it. Quick, effective, cheap. The same applies to your equivalent employees, i.e. the small, inexpensive, junior ones. They won't fit in a zip-lock plastic bag and stamping on them won't actually kill them, unless you really get stuck in (you'll need to put down newspaper though as this gets really messy), but the principle is the same. But the loonies in HR just don't go for this kind of approach. It's as if they are trying to be deliberately obtuse, denying the logical approach and instead insisting on pursuing this bizarre, fluffy road to ruin.

Staff training, succession planning, talent management and equality and diversity: these are the mantras of the HR 'professional'. If you're not careful, they will swallow all of your department's resources (time and money) and squander it all on expensive consultants and ridiculous events of one kind or another. They will agitate in your department to demand a Christmas party or a 'reward scheme'. They will tattle on you to their seniors, who, depending on the structure of your organisation, may be plumbed in to the very most senior of people in your company. They are downright dangerous and you just can't ignore the threat they pose to you, your future happiness and your future richness. You must see them clearly as your enemy. They will attempt to appear just like you, all hard and tough and keen to make 'tough decisions'. Don't be fooled, these are sheep in wolves' clothing.

I hope I have illustrated just how dangerous these sheep can be however and now we will look at ways of neutralising the threat that HR pose...

The first and most obvious way to stifle the voice of HR is with chloroform or a sharp blow to the back of the head. Either of these methods can be followed by a quick change of carpet (was the Axminster wearing a bit thin?) in your office facilitating a quick trip to the local dump or quiet canal. This approach does have its risks however, as if you do get caught, the police, while very understanding of your motives, will be compelled to try you for actual murder. In some countries murder comes in various degrees, for example:

- Cold blooded, first-degree murder.
- Provoked murder (murder in the heat of passion etc.).
- Manslaughter through a dangerous act.
- Accidental manslaughter.
- Murder in self-defence.
- Neutralisation of a combatant in warfare.
- Killing of a dog, cat or other pet.
- Murder of an HR professional.
- Stepping on a beetle.
- Swallowing a fly.

Under this system, the murder of your HR professionals might result in a stern rebuke, some serious tutting or some other proportionate admonishment, but it's wise to check before you take any further action. If the country of your residence ranks HR professionals alongside other human beings in terms of importance and status (a mistake clearly), then you need to come up with other approaches to reducing the burden they place on you. Based on the truism that the best form of defence is attack, let's look at what we can do to push HR over the edge.

The first thing to bear in mind is that HR people don't really do anything; they have probably never done a real day's work in their lives, so the thought of real effort is disproportionately scary to them. This gives you a huge advantage: you can become a *demanding customer*. As the saying goes, "Keep your friends close, and your enemies closer". Give your HR people lots and lots to do. This should all be busy work that you can keep at arm's length and away from interfering with the day-to-day work of your minions.

> The first thing to bear in mind is that HR people don't really do anything.

At the Terrible Leadership Research Institute, we have done some research using HR professionals to find out what things you can use to keep them busy and un-worryingly occupied. We hooked up their HR salivary glands (all HR professionals are born with these, and they are as a result more susceptible to colds and sniffles), so that we could measure their anticipatory response when given various vacuous forms of busy work to do. I'd like to point out here that all of the approaches we used were highly inhumane and many, many HR professionals were harmed, some quite badly, during this research. This was all great fun, and what we found was very interesting. The following projects were the most effective at encouraging HR types to gallop of on wild goose chases for upwards of a month:

- Strategic capability review.
- Full activity analysis and organisational design review.
- Training needs analysis.
- External benchmarking for salary review.
- Create and launch an employee opinion survey.
- Employee value proposition.
- Employee retention strategy.
- Redesign of a talent management process.

What you will notice about all of these is that they are strategic reviews, analyses or diagnoses. None of them is actually *doing* anything. This will give your average HR weirdo a degree of comfort, so they are more likely to gravitate to this kind of work. This is especially true if you tell them that you would value their strategic insight (snort!). In order to extract the maximum value from these 'efforts' set some really long and distant delivery dates. As they say, work expands to fill the time allotted to it, so give them six months for a training needs analysis, nine months for a full strategic capability review. Now, obviously, any sane, right-thinking individual would complete these tasks (if they can be called such) in a matter of hours or days, not months. But, the aim here is not to get these tasks completed, but to keep HR actively employed in essentially doing nothing. They will spend an inordinate amount of time in focus groups, and this can be a worry, as it is possible they will attempt to distract your minions in these focus groups. To prevent them from doing this you need to do two simple things:

1. Tell your minions in no uncertain terms that fraternising with HR will cost them their jobs.
2. Allow your HR person to recruit a bunch of other HR people.

This then gives HR a team to focus group with, and an organisation that doesn't want to talk to them. They will now find it so much easier to focus group each other than anyone else that they will do this repeatedly and contentedly until... well, we're not sure how long they'll keep this up for because a longitudinal study we started in the 1960s is still going strong. So, you can certainly buy a career's worth of HR faffing about with this sort of approach. Occasionally, they will want to talk to you about the results of this review or that analysis or another report. Much as you will want to vomit copiously on their inexpensive and unfashionable shoes, I suggest you respond warmly to these invitations. They will then present a bunch of nonsense that will be largely incomprehensible (if you look closely you can normally spot where they have edited out the pixies and flowers from their reports at the last minute).

Appear to listen and then come over very cautious and nervous. Use some of the following points to get the tone just right:

• People development is very important to you and you want to make sure you are only doing what is best practice.

- You are concerned about sending a consistent message and don't want to contradict anything that is being communicated to other departments.
- You have heard that other organisations are looking at this issue differently now, and that there is a new strategic direction being pursued by other leading organisations.

> The aim here is not to get these tasks completed, but to keep HR actively employed in essentially doing nothing.

Then thank them for the sterling work they have done so far and commend them on a commendable initial draft. Suggest a follow up in a couple of months. They will hurry off in a flurry of renewed activity. It is around about now that you need to layer on a new priority (refer back to the list of researched topic areas). Suggest that this is now your top priority and that whilst you don't want them to lose focus on the initial project, you'd also like them to start a... If you keep this up you should be meeting with your HR person every few months (about four times a year should do it). Now obviously, this is likely to bring you out in a rash, but by keeping it down to four times a year the rash should be mild, and controllable with some ointment.

So, there you have two methods for dealing with the threat that HR represent: murder and distraction technique. Personally I'm tempted to suggest that two perfectly good, well thought through options are enough, but for those of you who want more then here's another suggestion — professional undermining.

Professional undermining

This is probably the most complex and time-consuming approach to dealing with HR, but it has a certain flourish and élan that the Terrible connoisseur will appreciate. It is critical to recall that essentially HR is a non-job, so, HR credibility is a particularly flimsy and fragile affair. It is based more on time served in senior HR roles and in large, well-known corporations than on knowledge, track record or capability. HR credibility is like a delicate shadow of a normal business person's credibility. It is wafer-thin, and sheer so that you can normally see straight through it. Now, one might reasonably assume that this means it is easy to tear to shreds, but do not underestimate the human response to threat. Like with any muscle, the more of a pounding it gets the stronger it becomes. So while an HR person's credibility is wafer-thin they will typically, as a result, have become adept at defending it. If you attack an HR person's credibility it is like attacking a fox cub. You can expect the mother to come out fighting. Now a fox, like an HR person, is not an inherently dangerous animal and can normally be dealt with by a swift blow to the head with a stout stick. But, just like our analogous fox, the HR person can deliver a nasty bite. They're also quite mangy animals and you never know where they've been, or what they've been eating... have you had your HR person checked for rabies lately? Ok, maybe the analogy breaks down eventually, but you get the point. A straightforward attack is probably not the most sensible, subtle or even Terrible approach to take. No, if you really want to undermine their credibility, first you have to trick the mother fox into trusting you to take care of her fox cub for her...

Start by making sure your HR person receives lavish praise from you, especially around the time they are submitting or reviewing their endless, vacuous and meaningless reports and analyses with you. In their heads, you need to be their greatest admirer, supporter and they should feel like you trust them intimately with your gravest concerns. A good way of doing this is to confide in them some intimate personal details. Concerns about your personal finances, children, relationships, etc. all make good topics. Now, the trick is to keep these inconsequential (I think my husband is spending too much time with his buddies from work and not enough with the children, *or*, my wife spends too much on shoes and handbags). Making this something relatively personal makes them feel that you must really trust them and therefore encourages them to trust you in return. Now, obviously, you make these details up, you would never give them something they could in future use against you. Remember, you need to get them to trust *you*, obviously you don't trust *them* as far as you can throw them. On its own though, this won't be enough to get them to hand over to you their most valuable (some would say only) asset: their credibility. They won't choose to trust you fully until they feel confident that they can place themselves in a vulnerable position in the belief that you have their best interests at heart. Essentially, you are going to need to create such a convincing yet false sense of security that they fall into your trap. Sound difficult? Not really.

You see, the average HR person is not very bright and will fall easily into the following traps:

1. Find out about something they like (hiking, death metal music, crabs, scrabble, cross-stitch) and then send them something or get them something appropriate. You need to hit the 'I saw this and thought of you!' button. Any old article hastily torn out of 'Personnel Today' or equivalent will do, but consider the option of tasking one of your more hapless and useless minions to doing a bit of research and getting hold of something a bit more impressive.

2. Ask them about their family or personal life and then get one of your minions to write down some pertinent points to remember. Have the minion brief you about those points just before you go to see them again and ask them suitably fluffy questions: "How is little Jackie?" or, "Did you enjoy the skiing season?". It might make you retch a little to ask this kind of question so it is wise to make sure you go armed with a sturdy handkerchief in case you need to be a little bit sick. Do try and appear at least slightly interested in the mindless drivel this kind of enquiry will induce. A good question followed with a look of mind-numbed boredom will rather reduce the impact.

By now you have hit your HR person with a two-pronged assault. You have used disclosure (confiding in them) and other-centeredness (remembering things about them) to encourage them to trust you. This is normally more than enough to generate a deep level of trust between them and you and the mother fox has now been tricked into a false sense of security. She will no longer see you as a threat, indeed quite the opposite, and will respond warmly to the idea of you taking care of her cub. They will be saying positive things about you to their bosses and colleagues and it will appear that the two of you have a good positive working relationship. The trap is now set, all you need to do is look for your opportunity.

Try and find out if they are looking to get promoted, or if it would be helpful for them to get some customer feedback. What you are looking to engineer is an opportunity to talk to their boss about them privately. It doesn't work if you instigate this. If you do you will come across as a stroppy, disgruntled client and the HR person's boss will only half listen to you. You need to be invited to deliver your feedback. Your HR person will make it clear that they believe you have an excellent working relationship, and that they trust your judgment, so their boss will be expecting your feedback to be warm and cosy. So, when you're invited to meet the boss make it clear that you only have their direct report's best interests at heart, that you only want what is right for them. Then make it clear that what you feel would be best is re-assignment to cleaning dishes in the staff canteen. You will have lots of examples of the fact that they haven't delivered anything for you (this is because you haven't let them, but you can gloss over this). You can justifiably bemoan the fact that they always seem to be finding things out rather than doing anything. You can make it clear that whilst you like them personally (practice your best tone of sincerity for this — delivering this line through clenched teeth doesn't work so well), you suspect that they are rather out of their depth professionally. Then simply ask to schedule some time to talk to them in a month or two to talk about securing some more appropriate HR support.

And there you have it. You have now successfully torpedoed the entire career of your hapless HR moron. They will be moved, either to a new area, or out of the organisation entirely. Most likely they will be put on a central project team where they can't do any harm. Word will leak out that working with you is suicidal as the skewered corpses of HR careers pile up around your reputation. The sharper, more challenging HR types will give you a wide berth and only new, stupid or badly connected HR nutcases will be assigned to you, making HR an increasingly manageable and insignificant threat to you and your Terribleness. This is as close to impaling someone as you can get in most normal business environments these days. Granted, Vlad the Impaler wouldn't recognise it as a proper response to a perceived threat. But then Vlad lived in a much more literal time, where regular business practice involved treating enemies as giant pencil sharpeners. Vlad gave a whole new meaning to the term 'fundamentalist'...

By following the approaches and advice in this chapter, you can diminish the threat of HR, and perhaps even remove it completely. You will be free to let your Terribleness flourish and grow to its full monstrous capacity. Who knows where it will take you...

Chapter Ten — Lessons in Terrible

- Learn to recognise your enemies. HR is never your friend.
- There is in fact no such thing as Human Resources. It is a non-job.
- HR have a number of crazy ideas you need to be aware of and defend against:
    - 'staff training': wasting time and money to show your staff slides and pictures.
    - 'succession planning': wasting time and money planning who will take over from you (as if anyone could!).
    - 'talent management': wasting time and money trying to work out which of your minions is the least useless.
    - 'equality and diversity': wasting time and money by making it legally awkward to abuse minority groups.
- If murdering your HR nut-jobs isn't legally advisable then distract them by giving them mounds of meaningless work to do, e.g. employee value proposition.
- Tell your staff not to fraternise with HR, but do let them recruit their own people, thus encouraging them to only talk to themselves.

Chapter Ten — Lessons in Terrible

- Professionally undermine them, by first gaining their trust through:
  - disclosing some false personal details about yourself.
  - finding out and remembering some inanity about them.
- Then, once trust is gained, find a way of undermining them in front of their boss.

If you have gone to the not inconsiderable lengths required to create a Terrible leadership style and approach, you fully deserve to reap the rewards available to someone of your skills and determination. Don't let the reprobates in the HR department steal them away...

CHAPTER 11
A TERRIBLE LEGACY: CREATING A LASTING BLAME CULTURE

You have come a long way. When you picked up this book, you were probably under the misapprehension that leadership was all about flowers, fairies and rainbows. You have learned that to be a truly great leader you need first to become a Terrible leader. You have learned what being Terrible really means and have seen how Terrible leaders from history have used Terrible techniques to dominate their peers, achieve greatness and line their own pockets pretty successfully into the bargain. You have become masterful in the small things that go into becoming Terrible; you have begun managing the very real threat that your minions represent; and you have learnt how to keep those minions in a constant state of fear-fuelled frenetic activity. You have delved into a world of true power and how to abuse it and just when those meddlesome kids in HR thought they could thwart your Terribleness, you learned how to deal with them too.

You are now ready. Ready to pick up the mantle of Terribleness and wear it with pride. Congratulations, you have earned the respect, trust and friendship of your seniors, combined with the abject terror of your staff. This heady brew will serve you well and I feel totally confident in saying, "Go forth and conquer!" You have everything you need, so go and have some fun. When you have finished conquering for a few years, come back and read the rest of this chapter. You'll need at least three years of Terribleness under your belt before it makes real sense. But when you are ready to take the next step, remember that this chapter is here, because it can help you do something very special indeed. You can create your Terrible legacy…

Ok, you're back. How was it? People going green at the thought of an unexpected meeting with you 'to talk about the numbers'? Staff turnover at an all-time high? Empire built to staggeringly high numbers of people doing not much of any value? Motivation at an all-time low? People getting used to being beaten with office furniture? Good. You have been enjoying yourself evidently. If you can't honestly say 'yes' to most of these questions, then get back out there and don't come back until at least 5% of your staff are admitted annually to Accident & Emergency for 'stapler-related injuries'. And if you quibble, I'll make it 10%!

But for those who made it and have entered the hallowed grounds of practicing Terrible leadership I want to take you on your final Terrible journey. It will take you beyond yourself and beyond your own time. It will immortalise you. This journey requires much, much more than a series of practices and routines. It will not be enough to change your mindset. No. You must be ready now to examine your impact as a leader and as an individual at a much broader level. You cannot make this journey until your own inner Terribleness is at peace with itself. It should no longer feel like a conscious effort to ruthlessly sack someone who is getting a bit old, or to demotivate your employees to the point of suicidal despair. This inner state of Terribleness should be complete, at ease and natural to you. If this is the case, then it is time to go...

I want you to think about what people will say about you after you have passed away. Make a list of the things that you think might be said about you at your funeral, maybe not during the speeches, but in the private moments between those that knew you well. As a Terrible leader of some years' experience, I like to think my own list will be something like this:

> I want to take you on your final Terrible journey. It will take you beyond yourself and beyond your own time. It will immortalise you.

- He really understood what made people tick and then he'd stop it.
- He always saw mistakes as an opportunity to teach someone a lesson.
- He believed in equality; he treated everyone like shit.
- He didn't suffer fools gladly, but he did enjoy throwing sharp things at them.
- He saw the best in people and then had it removed.
- I'm still scared of him.
- Do you think he's really dead?
- If he goes to hell Satan is going to have a nightmare.
- He's bound to have done a deal to get into heaven, and then run it.
- I wonder what he's done with all his money?

- These are suspiciously good canapés...
- Shhh — what if he can still hear you...?

What will they say about you? Will the fear of your Terribleness reach out from the grave? Will the shadow of your awesomeness loom large after you have gone? What will be your Terrible legacy? As I approach the end of my Terrible leadership journey, now seems like the right time to consider how I will be remembered and how I can give something back to the society from which I have taken *so* much. I'd invite you to do the same. For me, part of my effort was to write this book so that Terrible leaders and aspiring Terrible leaders would have a guiding light, a beacon to guide them in the stormy froth of Sissiness. But you can't all go and write books about Terrible leadership, remember, I'm Terrible too, so you won't want to find out how I deal with competitors. And if you think you're more Terrible than me, then just remember — I wrote the book on Terribleness. So let's look at what else.

Because you are by now a true Terrible leader, there are really only three reasons why you would leave your post:
1. You get a promotion — congratulations.
2. You retire — congratulations.
3. You die — commiserations.

These will all feel subtly, ever-so-slightly different from your own personal point of view, but to the people you have been tyrannising up to that point it is all the same: you are leaving.

Soon they will have a new boss, a new working regime and a new way of life. Unless you think and act now all your hard work is about to be torn down by others. Now, I'm not a petty man, once I'm finished with something I'm not too worried about what happens to it, but if I've spent two hours building a sandcastle with all the turrets and a moat and buttresses and whatnot and I go for a swim only to see a couple of 15-year-olds jumping on it then...

So, were I to build a sandcastle I would be careful to fill it with used needles, broken glass and carefully sourced dog excrement. That way, when some feckless youths attempt to pull down my monument, they quickly learn that it bites back and they had best leave well alone or risk serious personal injury. Terrible leadership is like a sandcastle. Safe and sound and surprisingly durable, provided you are around to protect it, and lots of fun to build it up, but the moment you walk away, upstarts will stomp on it and the tides (of time) will wash it away. So, ask yourself: is your Terribleness something you are happy to see washed away, something to be expunged by a cavalcade of Sissy leadership? I say "no"! I want my Terribleness to linger long in the organisation where I constructed it, and beyond if at all possible. I want it to nestle, like a stubborn benign cancer, hugging the core of the organisation long after I have left, like a distinct entity with a life and mind of its own. I want, and I want you to want, a Terribleness that imbues the very organisational fabric with a sense of lurking dread, a degree of frenzied panic and a creeping feeling of personal fragility and ineptitude in the HR

> I want my Terribleness to linger long in the organisation where I constructed it.

department. This is our legacy to the world: a form of leadership so powerful that it sucks in power from all other sources to create a culture of oppression and despair all by itself. To achieve this you must reach out with your imagination (and feelings for the Jedi-inspired amongst you). Go to a place in the far future, 10, 20 or even 30 years after you have left the organisation. Look around you: see it, feel it, hear it and touch it (inappropriately if you like — imaginary Terribleness is good too). I want you to imagine that everyone is behaving as though you were the deity, as though they feared you and imagined your influence to be very real. What are they doing? What are they saying?

What you are envisioning is your Terrible legacy. These are the things people will be doing and saying if you can create a Terribleness that transcends time and your physical presence. This is advanced Terribleness that even some of history's most Terrible never truly achieved. To attain this level of Terribleness that goes beyond, you need to be organised. And you need to understand two things about organisational culture:

1. Culture is in the little things.
2. Once established, culture is very hard to change.
   It is durable.

In fact, culture is like a smart material. The harder you try and change it, unless you really know what you're doing, the more you will reinforce it. It is made up of thousands of tiny organisational habits, processes and 'that's just how we do things around here'. Some Terrible leaders understand this and build legacies that reach out for decades and even hundreds of years. Others don't...

Let's take for a case study the difference between Stalin and Hitler. How long did their legacies last after they were removed from power? In the answer to this question we can see the crucial difference in the capabilities between these two tyrants. Adolf Hitler is one of Terrible leadership's plucky triers. He had a good go at being a Terrible leader, but it was all a bit obvious, frenzied and short-lived. He was great at some aspects, particularly things like the management of minions and the ability to get a lot of frenzied activity from people. People were properly afraid of Hitler because he had a pretty well-known penchant for having people murdered nastily and brutishly (piano wire featured regularly). So he gets top marks there. But his Terribleness was ultimately unsustainable because he was too extreme and didn't create a lasting Terrible culture around him. This was partly because he didn't make any effort to slip in seamlessly to his surroundings.

The most dangerous threat is the one you can't see and as Terrible leaders we know that we need a degree of subterfuge to prevent the full extent of our Terribleness from coming to light. We should be like mushrooms: the bulk of us underground, with just the fruiting body pushing up from time to time to release some spores. Hitler wasn't a mushroom. (A point I made in my history exam aged 18: but history's loss is leadership development's gain.) Hitler didn't really go in for subterfuge. During the 1930s, especially the late 1930s when Hitler's armies began invading places, people were not all totally positive about the Nazi approach. To this day, it is fair to say that Nazism is not universally popular by any means. But too much of Hitler's Terribleness was tied up with the cult of his own personality; he was really Terrible, but not systemically Terrible. When he shot himself in Berlin in 1945, the Nazi party disintegrated almost instantly and Germany all but immediately capitulated to the Allies. Hitler's (and the Nazis') impact will last forever. His impact was huge, possibly more significant than any other recently deceased individual on the planet. But what is his legacy? Sure, he helped hasten nuclear proliferation (we'd have got there without the Second World War in all probability, but just slower), he ended the lives of millions and countless millions will therefore never be born. He helped galvanise the need for a Jewish homeland in Israel. He changed the world's views on euthanasia; there was the cold war, the Berlin Wall, etc. This is all pretty big legacy stuff, but the impact of his leadership culture evaporated at precisely the moment he pulled the trigger. There was an almighty and collective sigh of relief and Germans and Germany emerged blinking from the rubble of what was their country. If Hitler had been able to articulate his desired legacy he almost certainly would not have described the open, inclusive, peaceful, non-militarised, tolerant, balanced society that you find in Germany today. Whereas Russia on the other hand...

Stalin was no less Terrible than Hitler. He rose to staggering levels of power, was totally ruthless, killed millions etc. The only difference is that Stalin was far more methodical and only sensibly ambitious. Whereas Hitler wanted to... well, lord only knows what Hitler wanted, but from the way he set about it, we can only assume that he wanted to rule the world, Stalin was content to rule Russia (papers found after his death suggest he intended much more, but it is hard to tell whether he would have ever acted upon this). This is not to say he wasn't expansionist. Not since Ivan has Russia swallowed so much territory as it did during its Soviet period, with much of Eastern Europe falling under Moscow's influence. Stalin used all the usual tricks to ruthlessly dominate his rivals, his people and his minions. He divided and conquered so effectively he managed to maintain an almost constant state of frenetic competition.

But what Stalin did, and Hitler never managed, was to create a lasting legacy, a culture of Terribleness that survived until relatively recently in modern Russia (some would say it's still there today), and was certainly healthy until decades after his death.

He created a culture of secrecy. Under Stalin's direction almost everything was considered top secret. Directives in the secret Russian archives show that no decisions made by any of the senior committees were to be recorded. Just think about that for a moment. A country as large and as complex as Russia where critical policy decisions were not recorded on paper. Suddenly those with information become incredibly powerful and influential. And who ultimately has the information? The guy at the top, followed by those with access to him, and then those with access with the people who have access to him and so on and so on. The culture becomes one where information is power. Stalin, being Terrible, quite rightly mistrusted all of his minions and saw them for the very real threat they were. He therefore surrounded himself with a colossal bodyguard; indeed, he may have been the most heavily guarded leader in modern history. Eventually this bodyguard became his ruling party, as their proximity meant they were in reality the decision makers and power brokers of the USSR, privileged as they were to have access to what was critical: information and the will of 'the boss'. Stalin chose for his bodyguard normal people who were phenomenally loyal to him as a result of their sudden elevation from obscurity. In doing so, Stalin was following the legacy (possibly knowingly) of our hero Ivan the Terrible. Ivan had done exactly the same 450 years previously and the Guard of the Grand Prince has been a staple of Russian leadership ever since, even if the nomenclature has changed somewhat. Stalin removed all of the normal communication channels that existed in other countries. The press was silent, those in power could not get reliable, consistent information, responsibilities and accountabilities shifted like the sands. With total erosion of normal government, Stalin could be sure that his legacy would be safe for some time to come after his death.

> What Stalin did, and Hitler never managed, was to create a lasting legacy, a culture of Terribleness.

Stalin also created a culture of rivalry. His opponents were constantly pitched in battle against each other such that their energies were constantly blunted. The situation became so complex and intertwined that minions were often sent to execute their colleagues knowing full well that a similar fate awaited them at the hands of another. It is possible that by constantly revolving the framework of rivalry in his upper echelons, Stalin managed to create a level of learned helplessness amongst his more senior cadre. Learned helplessness was a phrase coined in the 1950s by a psychologist called Burrhus Skinner. He conducted a series of experiments with rats that went something along the following lines:

Step 1: Place rat in wire cage with a rubber-padded shelf.
Step 2: Sound buzzer and then pass electric current through cage — rat will immediately leap onto 'safe' rubber shelf.
Step 3: Repeat four or five times until rat is conditioned to jump onto shelf at the sound of the buzzer, and before the arrival of the electric shock.
Step 4: Remove safe zone.
Step 5: Continue with the buzzer and shock treatment four or five times.
Step 6: Reintroduce safe zone.
Step 7: Sound buzzer and the rat, rather than leaping for the reintroduced safe zone will just sit there and get shocked. It has learned helplessness.

Looking back at the behaviour of senior people in Stalin's regime, it looked as though they too had developed a certain learned helplessness through a prolonged exposure to brutal shocks. Disappearances became so common and expected that people even took to taking their own life rather than suffer the ignominy of being murdered. All the person sent to 'disappear' someone needed to do was turn up at their house in the evening, have a drink with them and say, "There is something you need to attend to in the other room". This was code for, "Step next door and shoot yourself, there's a good chap". And people did. There simply was no avoiding Stalin's whim. If he wanted you dead or removed, then that's what would happen, so best to take your own life rather than live with the uncertainty about how or when. One senior figure found himself unwittingly at odds with Stalin's will, but rather than attack him directly, a question was put to him about his wife's involvement with a group who were agitating for something or other. Of course, his wife had no such involvement but the guy quickly saw the situation for what it was and immediately confirmed that his wife was indeed an agitator. She was incarcerated in a military prison for years and treated terribly.

Stalin systematically broke the will of all the strongest leaders around him. He used rivalry, secrecy and complexity to create a system so anarchic and yet so totally controlling that people's ability to think rationally for themselves was permanently eliminated. The great thing about Skinner's box is that after the safe zone is reintroduced the rats don't jump for it — they have given up. This means that when you leave a legacy like Stalin's it lasts long after you have gone. Once broken, people don't mend and as a result Stalin's, and before him Ivan's, legacy reach out from their graves as stifling, terrifying and numbing as if they were still in the room. True terror, once felt, is never forgotten and lives with us forever.

> True terror, once felt, is never forgotten and lives with us forever.

This is how an organisational legacy is founded and established. Stalin progressed in his lifetime, as did Ivan before him, to an advanced, guru-like level of Terribleness. He knew that to ensure his legacy lasted he needed to change the behaviour, habits and culture of those around him. But what can we do to ensure that our Terrible legacy really has the legs to outlast our physical frailties? Let's look at an easy one to get us started...

Creating a lasting blame culture is one way in which you can ensure that long after you have left, for whatever reason, your name is still whispered with fear and respect. Blaming people for things is much more than just a fun thing to do to pass a long afternoon meeting. It serves a very real purpose as it distracts people from things such as why things happened, or how to prevent them from happening again. We don't really want our people focused on these factors. If they get to understand why things have happened, or how they can improve things in the future, there is a risk that they start to develop a sense of mastery and capability. This, as we know, is dangerous and to be avoided. So when things go wrong the first course of action across the organisation should be, *finding out whose fault it was*. Obviously, you will want to do this in order to teach someone a lesson, but you need to do more than this in order to create a legacy. Being a positive role model is great, but you need to change the behaviour of others. For instance, set up a process that is to be put in place after every major incident or error. Call this an 'after action review' or something, this will keep the HR ninnies happy. Create a detailed and consistent agenda to be followed at all after action reviews, perhaps something along the following lines:

1. Establish what went wrong, avoiding all discussion around *why* it went wrong.
2. Create an estimated cost in £/$ of the error.
3. Identify the most junior member of staff that can confidently be labelled as being responsible for the error.
4. Charge their boss with finding a way of extracting the cost of the error from them before firing them.

It is important to push responsibility for this kind of thing as far down the organisation as you can. You'll know when you've gone too low because it will be hard to ascertain whether it was their fault or someone else in their team. If this is the case then it's their boss's fault. Your job is to ensure that every single error is followed up by this process until it becomes a strongly inculcated organisational habit. Even if a Sissy leader rips out the process after you have gone, the muscle memory of assigning blame and retributive justice will be impossible to eradicate.

Creating a lasting blame culture is just one way in which you can create a Terrible legacy; there are many others. Consider creating a culture where:

- Illness is viewed as a firing offence.
- All people under the age of 25 are systematically harassed.
- Turning up late once results in having to work late for a month.
- Development conversations are strictly taboo.
- Communication between senior management and staff is restricted to a monthly haranguing about productivity.
- Employees' parents are brought in to discuss poor quality project work, regardless of whether they are deceased.
- People are assigned to projects on the basis of what they have specifically requested to avoid.
- All managers are expected to shout loudly and publicly to at least one member of staff per day.
- Employees suspected of establishing friendships at work are forced to exclusively wear corduroy.
- Employees who put photos of friends, family or pets on their desks are encouraged to bring in all their photos, which are then forcibly removed and shredded.
- Bullying people is seen as a positive part of working here.

To make any of these laudable cultural statements become reality you will need a process. For example, in the induction manual, there can be a set of instructions for managers on what to do if their new recruit brings in photos of their children for their desk. Or have all managers periodically and secretly observed for a day and if they don't shout at anyone they are summarily dismissed. These sorts of measures will convert good intentions into organisational routines and habits — and it is these that will live on long past your personal reign. Even if and when a Sissy leader stops managers being secretly observed, they won't know that this has happened (secrecy is so helpful). To them the world looks the same if they are being secretly observed of if they aren't. If you have taught them to learn helplessness, then they will carry on behaving as you have trained them even with the reintroduction of the 'safe zone', or Sissy leader in our case.

To do this effectively is difficult and challenging. It asks you to step back and observe your own organisation and think about what you can do to shape and mould the behaviour of countless, useless individuals. The trick is to see them for the lab rats they are. Their behaviour can be conditioned using stimuli. The sticks and dragons you have carefully crafted can be used, if applied repeatedly, consistently and methodically, to shape the behaviour of your people regardless of whether you are there in person or not. If you doubt this just remember, Stalin's minions killed themselves on his instruction, even if the man himself was hundreds of miles away. You can create complex, intractable organisational structures that duplicate responsibilities and blur accountabilities. You can create inordinately prolonged planning cycles so that uncertainty about investment priorities creates numbing paralysis. You can create internal competition between teams so that people fail to spot the real competition emanating from outside the organisation, and use that as an excuse for brutal measures to bring your organisation 'up to speed in the face of external benchmarks'.

You can do all these things and more and you will create a Terribleness that goes through and beyond your mere physical presence. By doing these things, you can warp the organisation to your Terrible tune and make it dance a stilted, crippled, inward-looking, self-harming dance that it may never fully recover from. In this form, it will create the perfect environment for you to draw from it everything you could possibly want and need, and it will be so tangled up scratching at itself that it won't notice, in fact, it will feel dependent on the very source of the poison you are injecting into it. It will flex to your will and succumb to your every whim, and when you are finished with it, it will attack anything that tries to straighten it out. Like a black hole, it will suck in everything around it, drawing from its environment a lurking, ominous power, giving nothing, taking everything. Genghis Khan created such a black hole and the Mongol hordes continued to sweep across Eurasia for 150 years after his death. Ivan the Terrible begat Stalin and the cold war that almost cost humankind its planet. They were the Terrible sources of power at the centre of these black holes. They were power personified. Edvard Radzinsky in his book on Stalin puts it perfectly, recounting Winston Churchill's remembrances of Stalin:

" *'Stalin made a very great impression on us... When he entered the conference room at Yalta we all stood up as if at a word of command.' Churchill also said that on one occasion he was determined not to stand up, but when Stalin entered it was if some extraterrestrial force lifted him from his seat."*

This is where the path to Terrible leadership leads. To the point where you only need enter a room and the most powerful people on the planet stand up in awed respect. Terrible leadership knows no bounds, no limitations. If perfected, it will take you as far as you want it to. The only question you will ever need to answer is how far do you dare to walk this path...?

Chapter Eleven — Lessons in Terrible

- Think about what you want people to say about you after you have left the organisation.
- Put dog poo in your sandcastle. Or to put it another way, create an enduring legacy that bites back if people try and pull it down.
- Culture is in the little things; take care of the details.
- Once established, culture is very hard to change — it is durable.
- Don't be like Hitler, be like a mushroom. Keep the majority of your Terribleness out of the sight of others. Careful subterfuge is an important part of creating a Terrible legacy.

Chapter Eleven — Lessons in Terrible

- Follow Stalin's example and create a culture that values secrecy and rivalry. Do this by keeping things secret and by setting up individuals and teams to constantly compete with each other.
- Create a culture of 'learned helplessness' such that your people learn that no matter what they do, bad things happen to them randomly and that there is no safe zone for them to retreat to.
- Aim to create a healthy blame culture where the organisation spends plenty of time self-flagellating. Make sure you establish a set of processes that are rigorously enforced and that these enshrine the allocation of blame.
- When you think about your legacy, you need to think about the process or system that you will leave behind that will carry your influence for months and years after you have left the building...

A dog is not for Christmas. It's for life. In the same way, Terrible leadership is not just for when you are here. It's for ever. And ever. Think now about how your influence will be felt by those who join your organisation long after you are being used as fertiliser...

part five

Learning
from the
Terrible
leader

One day I'm going to write a proper book on leadership. When my body is slowing down and I'm no longer interested in running around London. Or when a whisky by the fire with a dog at my feet seems like a better idea than a gut-full of ale and lots of roast lamb in the Anchor & Hope. But until then I think it's more fun to come at learning sideways. We've run alongside some really important ideas in this book, but we haven't tackled them head-on. We have been learning obliquely. But personally, I suspect that's how most learning happens. We do something we haven't given much thought to, it goes horribly wrong and people tut, and then we think, in a quiet moment, "What just happened there?"

And yet, you've forked out the money to buy this book and as I sit here now, I do feel I have short-changed you somewhat (unless you bought this second-hand or had it given to you, in which case you can stop reading now, you cheapskate!). So here's the deal: here you will find a condensed set of the lessons from the Terrible leader, switched around for ease of use so that you can take each lesson in its turn and digest them nice and easily. It may not be quite so much fun this way, but it might help to jog a few memories...

This is the learning from the Terrible leader without the use of the word 'minions'.

Terrible Lesson	Reversed
Chapter 1 Reclaiming Terrible (p21–31)	
We should covet the epithet 'Terrible'.	We should identify the core quality we bring to our leadership. We should know and understand the type of leader we wish to be.
It is safer to be feared than to be loved.	If they fear you, you have lost them.
Leadership is not a popularity contest, therefore it must be an *unpopularity* contest.	Granted, leadership is not a popularity contest. Great leaders work to understand what their people *need* in order to perform to their best and give them that. Sometimes what people need and what they want are different.
When punishing people, make sure to punish some extra, innocent people, to drive the point home.	We punish naughty children. Move out of this frame of mind when thinking about colleagues and employees. They are adults and don't need punishing unless they have done something illegal.
Beware Sissiness and Sissy leaders — but *don't* seek to put them right.	Terrible leaders are out there. Your support, coaching and advice can help them to become better leaders. *Do* intervene.
Nurture your desire for power and control.	Be cautious of your desire for power and control. We should seek to serve the people who follow us. They make the real magic happen. Accept accountability and support them to perform to their best.

Terrible Lesson	Reversed

Chapter 2   Making the case for Terrible leadership (p32–55)

Uncertainty and competition are the key ingredients for ensuring the appropriateness of Terrible leadership.	Clarity and collaboration are key ingredients for ensuring your people are able to perform effectively in modern organisations.
It is the job of the Terrible leader to increase the levels of uncertainty and competition so that our Terribleness (appropriate, but sometimes unpalatable) is found to be more acceptable.	Our role as leader is to support people to navigate through uncertainty by emphasising what is still true, by creating a world in which change happens without causing the stress uncertainty brings. It is our role to support our people in working together and to reduce internal competition when it detracts from the creation of value in our organisations.
Increase uncertainty by maintaining shades of grey in the organisation — try and prevent people achieving clarity about what it is they should do.	Be clear about people's roles, the expectations we have of people in roles, people's objectives etc. We don't have to set these ourselves: our experienced people will be able to do this for themselves. Our role is to work alongside them to ensure they are clear and confident about what they are doing.
Change your mind routinely and regularly.	Change the course of people's efforts only when you have to. When you have to, explain carefully why you have to. The fewer adjustments as to the direction of travel, the better. So, better to spend twice as much time up front in consideration and then make half as many course corrections.

Terrible Lesson	Reversed
Increase competition by setting up internal rivalries between individuals and teams — by dividing, by keeping people clawing at each other rather than us, we conquer.	Focus people on the goals and targets that they have in common in order to reduce friction and competition between teams. Where you see internal competition hampering performance, point it out and refocus people on new goals.
It is much easier to make others look bad than to make yourself look good.	Build on your own ideas and the ideas of others. Criticism is easy, but never wins friends. Don't build a reputation as the one who can always pick a hole.

Chapter 3 Lessons from History (p56–85)

Every mistake is an opportunity to teach someone a lesson.	Every mistake is a golden opportunity for people to learn. When they're ready and they've stopped beating themselves up about it, ask them gently and patiently if they'd like to try.
Keep track of your favourite punishments and hand them out on a rota system so that all of your hapless reports benefit from each in turn.	Keep track of your favourite ways of rewarding and recognising people and make sure you find ways of using them regularly.
If your control over a team, department or organisation is slipping, get it back by dividing and conquering. Use structure to set people up against each other.	If your control is slipping, bring people together and operate as a uniting force. Through you, people should find it easier to break down internal organisational boundaries.
Line your pockets.	Never steal from the organisation.

Terrible Lesson	Reversed
Play not to lose: destroy the things (resources) that you can't use but that others might otherwise advantage from.	Look out for opportunities to help others get ahead.
Make examples out of people to scare other people into behaving like you want them to.	Make examples out of the positive behaviour of others. When people do well, put them (with their permission) on a pedestal and celebrate their achievement.

Chapter 4 How Terrible are you? (p92–103)

Measure your innate Terribleness now, and then again every six months or so to track progress.	Collect feedback (e.g. 360) every six to 18 months to understand how people perceive your leadership capability. Use a mentor or another trusted person at work to collect feedback or to sound people out about your image occasionally to make sure you have an accurate self-image. Use a good quality psychometric (search online) to understand your innate leadership preferences.
Buy a leopard.	Don't buy a leopard.

Chapter 5 Towards Terrible day by day (p104–132)

Manage the conditions of your Terribleness — trip yourself up from time to time, get out on the wrong side of bed.	Manage your positive leadership impact. Be aware that your mood is infectious, and that if you look and feel miserable and angry, this will affect your people. Remind yourself of why you and your team should feel confident.
Make Terribleness a routine, schedule early morning rants to drive high performance.	Make celebrating success and thanking your team for their hard work a routine.

Terrible Lesson	Reversed
Complain — a lot, and wherever possible, unreasonably.	Be reasonable and evidence-based in your feedback. Only give feedback if you are well-intentioned about it, i.e. don't give feedback as a result of irritation or frustration, but instead out of a desire to support people to do better.
Manage your diary carefully, move people around at the last minute and catch other people unprepared.	Manage your diary carefully. Stick to what you've committed to do, be reliable and remember to follow up with people.
Walk the floor (or 'management by walking around' as the Sissies call it) and terrorise people as you go.	Walk the floor to find out how people are, what they are working on, what they're excited about. Have fun with people and find out more about them.
Never remember people's names, even when you do.	Make a real effort to remember people's names. It is the sweetest thing we can hear another person say.
Ask people difficult questions at random times and show obvious disapproval when they struggle to answer.	Ask people open questions that demonstrate you are interested in who they are and what they are doing.
Manage people's expectations, i.e. make sure they never get what they expect, keep them guessing and in a constant state of uncertainty.	Manage people's expectations, i.e. stick to your commitments so that people get what they have been promised. If you can't commit, don't commit and explain why you can't. Build certainty around what you can, explain why uncertainty exists where you can't and help people to manage that.

Terrible Lesson	Reversed
Tear down other's arguments rather than building up your own.	Show real interest in the arguments and positions of others and build your own arguments by linking them to the concerns and interests of others.
Turn up late and leave early.	Turn up in plenty of time and spend the time people need. Don't manage your diary unrealistically; make sure there is space in-between meetings and engagements.
Make the boss like you (but stab them in the back at the first opportunity).	Get to know your boss and find out from them how you can best support them. Never say anything about them you haven't already told them to their face.
Generate uncertainty around expected performance levels.	Generate crystal clarity around expected performance levels.
Never give specific feedback, except sometimes. But maybe not. Or...	Routinely give specific feedback. At least five times more positive than constructive.
Be suspicious of people who want to collaborate.	Work hard to find those who are keen to collaborate and take risks with them; demonstrate that you trust them.
Confuse and distract whenever possible.	Clarify and focus whenever possible.
Work to create a culture of blame.	Work to eradicate any existing culture of blame and instead work to create a culture that values performance.
Shout at people who leave early.	Shout (jovially) at people who stay late. Every night. As a result of not having been focused between 9–5. Or if you think they are trying to impress you.

Terrible Lesson	Reversed
Send very brief emails.	Send emails that are polite, yet to the point.
Get rid of sick people.	Support people who fall ill, and make sure there is nothing in the work place that can be managed that is making them ill. Treat people in this situation as you hope people would treat you.

Chapter 6 Authentic tyranny (p133–144)

Never show any weakness. Your staff must perceive you to be better than them at everything.	Be prepared to show (non-critical) weaknesses. You will gain your people's trust if they see you as someone who is able to ask for help, and who doesn't have all the answers.
Never let your staff get to know the real you. Remain aloof and mysterious, unless you want to frighten them.	Help your people get to know the real you. We work hardest for the people we trust. We trust the people we know, so let them know you.
Remind your staff that they are pond scum. Invest in all the small signals that remind them of their inferiority, such as a nice office and lush pot plants for you, and cheap, second-hand chairs for them.	Remove the signals that denote rank. Give up your personal office. Get rid of fancy titles. Encourage everyone to behave as if they were personally responsible for the long-term results of the company, i.e. encourage people to be seen and treated as equals.
You are physically, intellectually, morally and socially superior to your staff.	You aren't. So don't behave like you are.

Terrible Lesson	Reversed
Create a climate of high risk and low support for your people. If people do well, banish them. If people do badly, pressurise them. The ones that scrape along, just leave them alone and they'll be grateful.	Create a climate of high challenge and high support for your people. Create an environment where people understand the risk appetite of the team/department/ organisation and are incentivised to try new things. If people do badly, congratulate them and encourage them to learn why. If people do well, congratulate them and encourage them to learn why, i.e. "If you can meet with Triumph and Disaster and treat those two imposters just the same".
Measure how much you enjoy random acts of Terribleness to track your level of authenticity.	Keep track of how enjoyable you find management and leadership tasks to check that you are learning to derive intrinsic motivation and pleasure from being a leader, as opposed to an individual contributor, i.e. don't become a frustrated manager who desperately wants to be 'hands-on' and meddle.
You have to be authentic through and through, it can't be a style you adopt for nine hours a day.	Actually, ultimately, that's true. Leadership is about who you can become. Not what you can do. It may not start out that way, but if you're going to make a long-term career out of leadership (it may span 40 or even 50 years after all), then it's true.

Chapter 7 Making them miserable (p149–180)

Your useless minions, despite looking harmless and ugly, are in fact your greatest threat and need to be managed as such.	Your highly-skilled team are your greatest asset. Their capability and success *is* your success. They are how you will be measured.

Terrible Lesson	Reversed
Reduce empowerment by eliminating all clarity around objectives by following SCAB methodology.	Ensure objectives are clear. Check the basics by looking back at the SMART mnemonic.
Prevent people from developing any skills or capabilities by preventing them from attending training and by moving them around a lot.	Encourage people to learn using an approximate ratio of 70:20:10. Seventy per cent of learning should come on the job, where it is your job to position work/projects and encourage reflection around performance. Twenty per cent should come from relationships such as coaches or mentors. Ten per cent should come from training. Move people around to encourage them to build skills, and allow people to establish a sense of mastery before moving them on again. Move highly-talented people around regularly; your very best will be bored in most roles before two years are up.
Erode self-belief by being relentlessly critical.	Foster self-belief by relentlessly building the confidence of others.
Practice low empathy in order to avoid finding out how people are feeling: never ask questions and ask people to shut up.	Practice high empathy to find out how people are really feeling. Ask good, open questions and never tell people to shut up.
Prevent a sense of engagement emerging by disconnecting people's efforts from meaningful results.	Encourage a sense of engagement by connecting people's efforts directly to visible and meaningful results. If people can't see the connection, take them to where the impact of their work is felt and show it to them.

Terrible Lesson	Reversed
Help your staff see the customer (internal or external) for the naive, unrealistic, selfish people they really are.	Help your staff to understand the needs, desires and concerns of customers more deeply. Make the customer real to every person in the company.
Reduce energy by keeping people spread out in the office, closing the gym and discouraging people from cycling to work.	Increase energy by keeping people working together in relatively close quarters where information and news is easily disseminated. Encourage people to live and eat healthily. They will be more alert, feel better and work smarter.
People with too much energy are incredibly dangerous.	People with too little energy are less productive. Find ways of helping people to bring more of themselves and more of their full energy to work.
Use HR-administered surveys to check the level of engagement or empowerment is low.	Use surveys to check on levels of engagement and empowerment and then engage staff on what they'd like to see change in order to improve it.

Chapter 8 Motivation for Terrible leaders (p181–214)

Terrible leaders balance grinding their employees' morale into the dust with maintaining a frenetic level of well-targeted activity.	Good leaders know that high employee morale will in and of itself contribute to high levels of well-targeted activity.
In the game of carrot and stick, stick always wins. People move away from unpleasantness more quickly than they move towards nice things.	Throw the stick out. Clarity of purpose, a sense of *why* something is important and the promise of getting better at something will work much better to create a sense of motivation.

Terrible Lesson	Reversed
Find out what your employees really like and then threaten to take these things away.	Find out what really motivates your people and then work out how they can get more of those things.
Category One: the *workers* like clear targets and challenging goals. Threaten to remove any goal they've created and dangle the false carrot of promotion just in front of their noses to create years and years of furious industry.	*Workers* (McClelland calls them 'Achievers') do like clear targets and challenging goals, so give them plenty of each. Be very cautious about the false carrot of promotion with *all* your people. Just occasionally ask them to slow down, reflect and to extract some learning from what they have just done, and make sure they learn to celebrate their achievements with the rest of the team.
Category Two: the *softies* like team harmony and meaningful relationships (whatever they are). Threaten to set them in competition against each other, work alone or to make some redundancies and just watch the work rate soar. If that fails, shoot some baby deer.	*Softies* (McClelland calls them 'Affiliators') do like team harmony and meaningful relationships, so again, give them plenty of both. Encourage them to collaborate and work together. Plenty of team lunches (these can be as work-focused as you like) will help. Remember, this group will work as hard, if not harder, than any other, if they feel they are working to something that matters to the team. And if you have to work the deer into this, then visit a petting zoo together. And shoot nothing.

Terrible Lesson	Reversed
Category Three: the *slicks* like to work on high-profile projects with more senior people. Threaten to consign them to the gulag of projects or to remove previously conferred 'special' advisor status. Award them meaningless changes to their title to make them feel more senior and executive, give them a bigger pot plant and they'll bust their balls.	*Slicks* (McClelland called them 'Influencers') do indeed like high-profile projects and the opportunity to work with senior people, so be sure to give them plenty of both. Be careful to ensure they are good planners and organised enough to be really impressive when they do eventually get on stage. Help them to keep the 'Bambi on ice' moments as few and far between as possible.
	No Terrible lesson to reverse here, but a key one is to remember that not all people are motivated in the same way that you are. Avoid the trap of assuming that what works for you will work for others. Sometimes, but far from always.
In the land of the dragon and the princess, princes do more running around because of the dragon, i.e. the burning platform will inspire more focused activity than the most well-honed of inspiring visions.	The burning platform excites so much activity, but people become tired and frustrated with constant crises. For more sustained, positive, revitalising urgency, you're going to need that princess.
Dragons are rarely called Simon. Or Nodgar.	Sadly true.

Terrible Lesson	Reversed
To generate truly furious levels of activity, you need at least three dragons to instil the required level of fear and dread in your employees.	To generate truly furious levels of activity, you need a vision of the future that genuinely inspires your people. It must be something that they want to make true.
To become your own best dragon, shout loudly at people.	There is almost never any call to shout at people. Unless they're about to be hit by a train, in which case shout all you like.
Swear at people.	Bad language is relative. You'll understand the culture of your organisation if you've worked there a while, but if you're new check before you cuss. Don't swear to fit in, but equally don't stop swearing (gently) once you become a leader in some effort to appear saintly!
Get in people's faces.	Don't invade people's personal space.
Physically intimidate people.	Don't! Be aware of the power of body language. Use yours to demonstrate confidence combined with humility.
Spit at people.	If you need telling this isn't a good idea...
Grow a large pair of buttocks.	Errrr..... struggling with this one. How about: there is no known correlation between leadership capability and buttock size? So your buttocks are fine, whatever the size.
Turn yourself red in order to appear more intimidating by holding your breath.	Just don't do this.

Terrible Lesson	Reversed
Use fear of the competition, your boss, redundancy, pay cuts or of failure itself to stimulate a higher work rate.	Rely on enthusiasm and energy to drive work rates, not fear. However, do encourage routine benchmarking against external competition, and build confidence internally that you can match or beat whatever you find out there.

Chapter 9   Power and its abuses (p215–241)

Now that you've attained a Terrible reputation and the resultant fear and respect that is due to you, *use it*!	Now that you are in a position of leadership, treat the role itself and the resultant accountabilities it brings with care, respect and humility.
Ask yourself not what you can do for your people, but how much of their bonus should they give to you? After all, they are only being awarded a bonus because of your well-honed and masterful motivational techniques, so doesn't it belong to you in the first place?	Don't even think about it. Also, don't get caught up in the belief that a person's bonus is the main component behind their motivation. It isn't, and not a single scientific study has ever found a connection between size of bonus and level of motivation for the job. In fact, all the science seems to suggest precisely the opposite, i.e. high bonus payments drive the following: "If you have to bribe me this much to do this job, the job itself must be intrinsically pretty shitty."
Not getting enough of the bad thing at home? Screw the graduates, or anyone else who tickles your fancy. But remember, after you've got them in the sack, to give them the sack shortly afterwards.	Be Very Careful. It might feel like falling in love to you at the time, but what *could* it look like to an employment tribunal if everything goes belly up in a few months. Many people meet their husbands and wives at work, so don't think for a moment that business and pleasure can't mix. If in doubt, stick to those whose careers you couldn't really affect even if you tried your hardest.

Terrible Lesson	Reversed
The company expenses system is a gold mine in the right hands. It is worth setting up a mining team.	Do it and watch your career go up in smoke!
Make sure suppliers know you're bribe-able.	Be purer than the driven snow. If even in the slightest doubt don't accept it, go halves or make sure all payment is personal and not being recharged, e.g. for tickets to sporting events. You can have friends who are also suppliers, but the question to ask is this, "Would we be doing these cool things together if we were paying ourselves?" If the answer is no, then you shouldn't be doing them.
Use your truly useless employees to do the things you don't want to. They won't complain, and if they do, they are the easiest to fire on grounds of gross incompetence.	If you have 'truly useless' employees then you should already have managed them out of the organisation having been very clear around expectations, given opportunity for development, clear feedback and had them on a performance improvement contract. In life, it is never a good policy to ask people to do things you would not be prepared to do yourself. Your parents will have cleared up your shit at some point, so if it's good enough for them...
Get involved in charities. They are a great place to siphon company funds into for a rainy day.	Get involved in charities which have a meaningful connection to the work you do. It's not only the right thing to do, it will encourage greater levels of engagement and motivation, which is good for productivity too.

Chapter 10 Pushing HR over the edge (p247–270)

Learn to recognise your enemies. HR is never your friend.	All the functions are your friend! Learn how to involve them in your work and how to make the best use of your organisation's skills in achieving your targets.

Terrible Lesson	Reversed
Staff training is wasting time and money to show your staff slides and pictures.	Staff training, whilst not the main source of learning by a long way for your people, can be an important way for people to learn new skills and approaches.
Succession planning is wasting time and money planning who will take over from you (as if anyone could!).	Succession planning is a vital way of managing organisational risk by ensuring a smooth passage from leader to leader.
Talent management is wasting time and money trying to work out which of your minions is the least useless.	Talent management is an important tool for sharing information about talented people across organisations, helping people to move between teams in order to build successful people to lead the organisation in the future. If done properly, it can also help us as leaders to ensure we are focusing on the right sorts of activities to develop every single one of the people in our teams.
Equality and diversity is wasting time and money by making it legally awkward to abuse minority groups.	The world is getting smaller. We are *all of us* in one minority group or another. Treat people equally. Look past diversity with a big 'D' (race, gender, sexuality, age etc.) and get really interested in diversity with a little 'd' (point of view, experience, style, mindset etc.). The most successful businesses have lots of diversity in terms of little 'd' (big 'D' diversity won't make you successful in and of itself). The fascinating thing is however, that big 'D' diversity and little 'd' diversity are nearly always correlated. And it's hard to see little 'd' diversity, so a quick and easy way of cheating is to make sure you've got plenty of big 'D' diversity — this normally does the trick.

Terrible Lesson	Reversed
If murdering your HR nut-jobs isn't legally advisable then distract them by giving them mounds of meaningless work to do, e.g. employee value proposition.	Murder no one! Involve HR, IT, Finance, Risk, Compliance (etc.) in the really big, tough questions you face in your business. You have capable resources around you that can help you — use them! Oh, and by the way, a clear value proposition articulating to the market why people should want to come and work for your company... that's pretty important stuff.
Tell your staff not to fraternise with HR, but do let them recruit their own people, thus encouraging them to only talk to themselves.	Encourage silos and boundaries between teams, functions and department to be broken down. Encourage a ferocious level of collaboration.
Professionally undermine them (HR) by first gaining their trust through disclosing some false personal details about yourself, and finding out and remembering some inanity about them.	*Do* gain people's trust by disclosing real information about you, who you are, what you hope for and what worries you. Find out and remember what matters to others.
Once trust is gained, find a way of undermining them (HR) in front of their boss.	Never undermine people in front of their boss, instead go out of your way to work out how to share people's successes.

Terrible Lesson	Reversed

Chapter 11 A Terrible legacy: creating a lasting blame culture (p271–289)

Think about what you want people to say about you after you have left the organisation.	Actually, I've messed up here, this is actually sound advice — do think about this, but just with a positive, non-Terrible slant.
Put dog poo in your sandcastle. Or, to put it another way, create an enduring legacy that bites back if people try and pull it down.	Your legacy should be more positive than this, how can what you strive for today keep giving back to your organisation and its stakeholders for months and years to come?
Culture is in the little things; take care of the details. Once established, culture is very hard to change — it is durable.	Absolutely true. Some senior leaders become obsessed with remaining strategic, thinking that they shouldn't get caught up in the detail. This isn't quite true. Great leaders understand that most detail does not require their focus or attention, but that the few details that are connected most directly to their strategic ambition, they need to be sweated over relentlessly. So great leaders do sweat the small stuff, but only the very small percentage of small stuff that matters disproportionately highly.
Don't be like Hitler, be like a mushroom. Keep the majority of your Terribleness out of the sight of others. Careful subterfuge is an important part of creating a Terrible legacy.	Ok, really, don't be like Hitler, that's fine to stay as it is. But don't conceal what you are doing from others. Be open and transparent about what you are doing and focusing on. Otherwise you run the risk of sliding towards game-playing.

Terrible Lesson	Reversed
Follow Stalin's example and create a culture that values secrecy and rivalry. Do this by keeping things secret and by setting up individuals and teams to constantly compete with each other.	Create a culture that values openness and collaboration. Do this by role modelling these values yourself and establishing norms or routines that embed them into the fabric of your team, e.g. a weekly meeting where challenges are shared and people are asked to collaborate on creating solutions together. This will endure long after you have left.
Create a culture of 'learned helplessness' such that your people learn that no matter what they do, bad things happen to them randomly and that there is no safe zone for them to retreat to.	Battle tirelessly a sense of 'learned helplessness' by giving people a sense of control and self-determination about what happens to them. If there is already a helpless culture in your team, then start with the small things; give people control over where they sit, then how they organise their working patterns, then their prioritisation of tasks and so on...
Aim to create a healthy blame culture where the organisation spends plenty of time self-flagellating. Make sure you establish a set of processes that are rigorously enforced and that these enshrine the allocation of blame.	Aim to create a healthy learning culture where the organisation spends plenty of time learning both from what went well and what didn't. Make AAR (after action review) an accepted and normal practice.
When you think about your legacy, you need to think about the process or system that you will leave behind that will carry your influence for months and years after you have left the building...	Damn it! That's good advice again. Add positive intention and you're looking good.

And there you have it.

96 reversible lessons from the dark side of leadership.

If you can just not do what the Terrible leader would do, you are half-way to becoming a great leader.

The next challenge is to think about what to do...

ABOUT THE AUTHOR

DAN WHITE is a leadership and management development consultant. He has designed and run courses and programmes attended by thousands of leaders from across Europe, North America, Africa, the Middle East, Japan, India, China and more. He was a Learning & Organisation Development Director at GlaxoSmithKline (GSK) before setting up his own consulting practice and writing books. He has himself been a leader in a large leadership development consultancy. He lives in London with his wife and daughter.

To contact Dan, visit his website at:
www.pangolinlearning.com